Flavours of New Brunswick

more recipes from our kitchens

by

Karen Powell

Edited by Susan Flood

Flavours of New Brunswick – more recipes from our kitchens

Neptune Publishing Company Ltd.
Printed in Canada 10 9 8 7 6 5 4 3 2 1
Design, Typesetting, Cover Photo – Paul Evans, Evans Communications Inc.
Additional Photography – André Gallant, Paul Evans
Editor – Susan Flood

Also by Karen
"A Taste of New Brunswick, recipes from our kitchens"
August 2001 Neptune Publishing Company Ltd. ISBN: 1-896270-17-4.

Library And Archives Canada Cataloging In Publication
Powell, Karen Elaine, 1967-
Flavours of New Brunswick – more recipes from our kitchens/by Karen Powell
Includes index.
ISBN 1-896270-41-7
1. Cookery, Canadian-New Brunswick style.
2. Cookery – New Brunswick. I. Title.

TX715.6.P687 2005 641.59715'1 C2005-902223-X

Sections

Acknowledgement

The words of kindness, and feedback on the taste and ease of the recipes from my first cookbook *"A Taste of New Brunswick, recipes from our kitchens"* (ISBN: 1-896270-17-4) was so very humbling to say the least. Your hunger for more simple, quick and tasty recipes in the form of a second cookbook has led to this wonderful title you are now reading. Without your constant inquires as to when my next book would hit the shelves, this book would not have been possible. I thank you for believing in me.

This book explores the food of New Brunswick that has fed so many of us and doubles as a tribute to the many farmers and fishermen who make NB their home. Where they eat the food they grow and fish, and invite us into traditions that are celebrated with the scrumptious food our gracious earth and water has given us. I hope you find as much delight in the fresh fruits, berries, vegetables and seafood that are not only bountiful in our region but also sustain many a livelihood and industry.

During my research for this book, I learned so much more than I knew was out there about our wonderful province New Brunswick. I met and spoke with many locals, listened to stories about family gatherings and festivals, talked recipes with everyone. The comradeship, the food, the celebrations, made me proud to call New Brunswick my home and to share with you, all the beautiful food and cultures within our reach.

Life is short; we never know how long we have so live every day to the fullest. Enjoy food with your family and friends, cherish the memories created. Take time to smell the apple pie from down the road at grandma's house. Food is life, celebrate it. I love to cook, I love to share food, and I love to talk with friends and family. Sharing a meal is the best way to have it all in life, good food, good friends, and good conversation results in great times and wonderful memories.

I can never say thanks to my family and friends enough, for all life's experiences we have shared and for the opportunity to share my cooking passion with them. Their help and words of praise made this book a reality.

This great province of ours will tempt you with its historical dishes and local favourites. Acadians from southern NB have two favourites which you must try called rappie pie (paté à la rapture) and poutine rapee (potato dumplings). Then there is bar clam stew another local favourite. Dessert stands out more due to the many creative ladies who stayed at home and produced wonderful delights for their families each day. Try to find a festival serving pudding in a hole (poutine-a-trou) or buttermilk pie (tarte-au-lait-de-beurre), or Acadian Chicken Fricot. Some of these recipes are contained here in this book. Enjoy!

New Brunswick

New Brunswick is approximately 74,000 sq. kms. or 29,000 sq.miles and we are happy to boast about its forested area still covering 2/3 of the land. The capital city is Fredericton. Other popular destinations are Saint John, Moncton, Bathurst, Campbellton, Edmundston and many more. New Brunswick is Canada's only official bilingual province. The time zone is Atlantic Daylight Time (ADT).

New Brunswick's Coat of Arms links the province to England. Through the lion; it celebrates the maritime region of shipbuilding. It was assigned by Queen Victoria in 1868 and in 1984 by Queen Elizabeth 2nd.

The provincial flag was born from the coat of arms and proclaimed in 1965. The golden lion on a red field across the top and a galley with its oars outstretched across the bottom of the flag is the basic design. The gold lion represents the triple gold lions of England. Our name derived from the Duchy of Brunswick in Germany from 1784. The heraldic ship reflects the growth and daily involvement of the sea in our culture, such as shipbuilding, fishing and travel.

Birds cover NB's fine coasts, inland waters and thrive in our great forests. The black capped chickadee was proclaimed the official provincial bird in 1983. The chickadee has a lovely song voice announcing spring with its songs of "chickadee-dee-dee" and "phe-be", "phe-be-be". The bird's colourful characteristics of a black cap and bib, white puffy cheeks help visitors and bird lovers alike to spot it easily during bird watching tours.

The Tartan of NB, designed by the Loomcrofters of Gagetown, NB, was officially designated in 1959. It is registered with the Court of The Lord Lyon, King of Arms in Scotland. The dark green represents our forestry, the meadow green is for agriculture, the blues reflect both coastal and inland waters, and the red represents the loyalty of early settlers and the Royal NB Regiment. These colours are all interwoven with gold to show the potential wealth of the province.

Flowers grow fragrant and robustly in our acidic soils, cool summer nights and hot days. The provincial flower is the purple violet. It usually grows in marsh-like areas. Its flowers grow high above its leaves at the top of the plant so the flower is there for all to see with its bluish purple flower gleaming in the afternoon sun. The flower is 3/4 to 1 inch in diameter, and grows about 5 to 10 inches in height. You can see them bloom across the lands from April through to June. It is native to NB and was adopted as the official flower in 1936. Another flower famous for its colours is the Lupin, a wildflower or weed as some locals refer to it. It is a long stemmed multi-budded cone that blooms with incredible fragrance and colours in every farm field and roadside throughout the province in spring.

New Brunswick is the largest of Canada's designated three Maritime Provinces, NB, NS, and PEI. The eastern boundaries are coastal with the Gulf of St. Lawrence and the Northumberland Strait. It is dotted with many fishing villages and sandy beaches. The other edges rest with the Bay of Fundy, which is famous for the highest and wildest tides in the world carving spectacular images along the coastlines.

How to Use This Book

A recipe is simply a guide for cooking, and is not written in stone. Start out by reading a recipe to be certain that you like all of the ingredients and that the ingredients are stocked in your pantry. Get all of the ingredients ready, vegetables cleaned and cut up. Cooking utensils should be set out and herbs, spices measured and any special tools or dishes ready. Always have your cooking surface pre-lined or pre-greased if needed. Everything should be on hand before you start to cook.

It may happen that there is a spice, herb, cheese or meat listed in a recipe that is not your favourite. Just replace it with the food of your choice that is of similar texture and consistency.

Food is best when it is fresh, so always use the freshest vegetables, fish, meat and herbs. Be careful not to leave perishable food out too long. Use clean kitchen etiquette to keep food fresh and to abolish any chance of food poisoning.

Some recipes can be adjusted to be fat free or low in fat, but some just don't taste the same without that heavy cream or that extra tablespoon of butter. If that is the case then choose another recipe to try if you are watching your fat intake or reduce the fat in other elements of the meal.

All of my recipes are in regular cups and pound measurements.
For those who prefer to use metric measurements, there is a page of conversion at the end of this book.

Flavour is the key to good food. With ripe fruit and vegetables; fresh cuts of meat; and fish, you can't go wrong.

Stock is another important factor and I have included recipes for all types of stock so you can muster the most flavour out of your food.

There are some basic sauces I have laid out that can enhance your cooking with less work than you expect. Try them for ease and convenience.

Chapter One

Vegetables

Down the garden path

VEGETABLES

Chapter One

Lemon Thyme Roasted Tomato Sauce

2 lbs.	tomatoes*
1/4 cup	olive oil
1	lemon (whole)
zest	of one lemon
1 tbsp.	thyme
1 tsp.	basil ground
	salt & pepper to taste

1. Cut tomatoes in half and place them in a shallow baking dish.
2. Seed and cut lemon into 12 pieces, place them amongst the tomatoes. Set aside.
3. In a bowl mix the basil, thyme and zest, together with the oil and then pour over the tomatoes.
4. Bake at 325°F until the tomatoes are soft, about 15 to 45 minutes depending on how hot your oven is.
5. Let cool. Remove and discard lemon except for 1 lemon wedge.
6. Place everything into a food processor and purée for 4 minutes. You can strain through a fine sieve for a smoother sauce. Serve warm or cold.

Suggestions: Use as a marinade; a basting sauce, pizza, bruschetta or as a dip. Chicken and potatoes baked in this sauce are out of this world.

Makes 2 cups.

* Tomatoes can be of any variety, such as baby, plum, beefsteak, cherry, heirloom, or field. The quantity and size of the tomato will change based on what variety you use. Different tomatoes have different amounts of seeds, juice, and pulp. Experiment with what you find in your area. I prefer the plum variety for this recipe.

Warm Wilted Summer Garden Spinach Salad

2 lbs.	baby spinach
1/2 lb.	bacon
1 cup	sweet onion finely minced
1 cup	wild rice
2 cups	mushrooms sliced thin
1/4 cup	balsamic vinegar
	salt & pepper to taste

1. Prepare rice according to package directions. Cool rice. Fluff with a fork. Set aside.
2. Clean spinach and tear into bite size pieces.
3. Place spinach in a deep bowl, add rice and toss. Set aside.
4. Fry bacon until crispy. Drain off grease, but reserve 1 tbsp.
5. Break bacon into small pieces. Sprinkle bacon into spinach and rice mixture.
6. Using the reserved 1 tbsp. of bacon grease, fry the onion and mushrooms until golden.
7. Pour the hot onion and mushroom mixture over the spinach rice mixture, toss well.
8. Drizzle balsamic vinegar over salad, re-toss and serve.

Serves 4-10.

Roasted Tomato and Onion Salad

3 lbs.	tomatoes*
3 lbs.	sweet onion**
1/4 cup	clarified butter recipe (page 69)
1/4 cup	olive oil
1 tbsp.	basil
1 tbsp.	garlic minced
1 tsp.	dried oregano
1 tbsp.	white sugar
	salt & pepper to taste

1. Cut tomatoes into pieces no bigger than 2 inches.
2. Cut onion into 1 inch pieces.
3. Place everything except the sugar into a shallow baking dish and toss well to ensure it is mixed evenly.
4. Sprinkle with sugar.
5. Bake at 325°F for 1 hour or until the onion starts to turn golden brown, stirring every 15 minutes.

* Tomatoes can be of any variety, such as baby, plum, beefsteak, cherry, heirloom, or field. The quantity and size of the tomato will change based on what variety you use. Different tomatoes have different amounts of seeds, juice, and pulp. Experiment with what you find in your area.

**Onion: Use sweet onions, like red, vidalia, or white.

Suggestion: Goes great over hot bread of any type, as a side dish, a topping for pizza or as a salsa.

Serves 6-12.

Vegetables

Did you know that potatoes cover 60,000 plus acres of New Brunswick? We grow more than 250 varieties and export to more than 35 countries. Potatoes are New Brunswick's largest income crop. Much of New Brunswick's potato success is attributed to the local climate, and soil. Potatoes are the fourth largest food crop in the world. In 1845 William Watts of Fredericton registered his patent for his potato picker invention. Farmers worked hard trying to save themselves time and money with inventions to make potato farming easier. Farmers had it hard in 1940 when the worst hail storm in history caused kilometers of damage and crop loss, with Saint-Andre de Madawaska the worst hit.

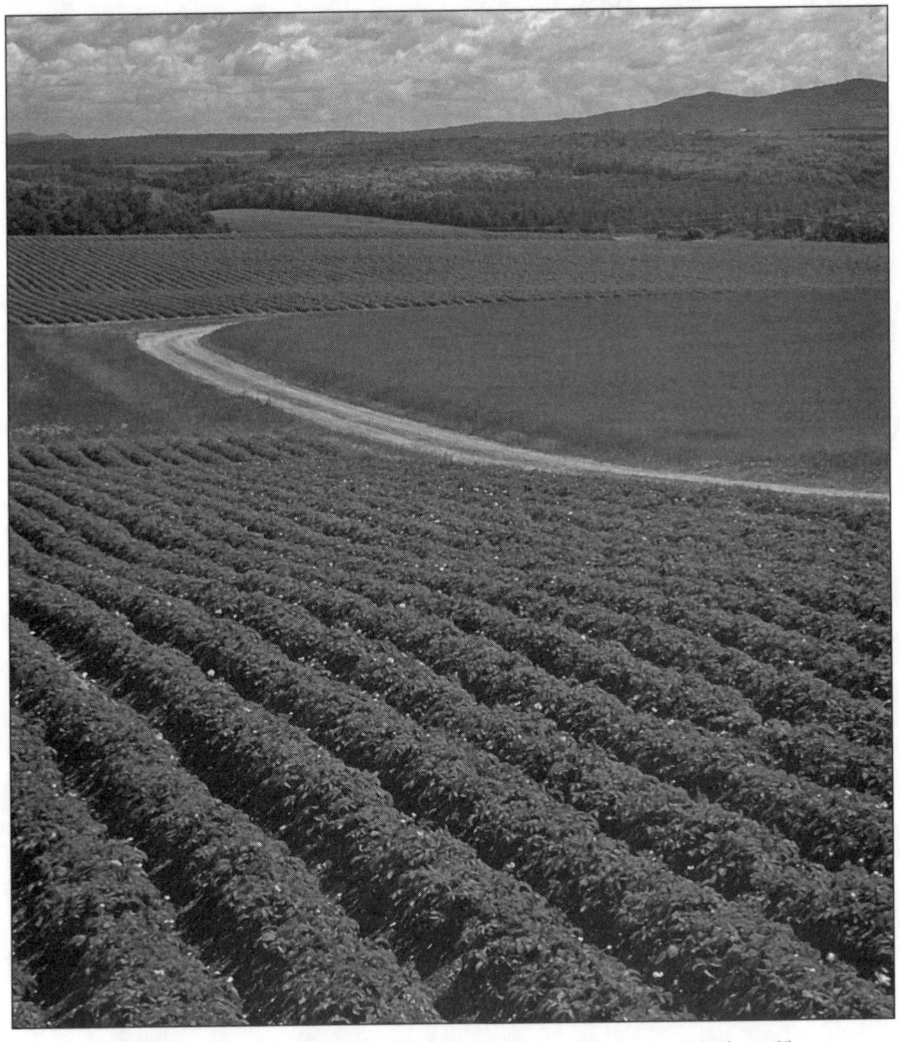

Potato fields, Drummond, NB. Photographer: André Gallant

Chapter One

Greek Mustard Salad

This salad requires fresh garden herbs, dried herbs cannot be substituted.

1 cup	small tomatoes* halved
1 cup	red onion finely diced
1/4 cup	oil soaked sun-dried tomatoes finely minced
1 cup	black olives sliced
1/4 cup	basil leaves
1/4 cup	mint leaves
1/4 cup	coriander leaves
1/4 cup	oregano leaves
1/4 cup	parsley leaves
1 head	romaine lettuce
1 lb.	baby spinach
1 cup	artichoke hearts chopped loosely
1 cup	mustard sauce (page 15)
	salt & pepper to taste

1. Tear herbs into bite size pieces and toss well in a deep bowl.
2. Add remaining ingredients and pour 1 cup Mustard Sauce over all (see recipe page 15). Toss until coated.

* Tomatoes can be of any variety, such as baby, plum, grape, pear, beefsteak, cherry, heirloom, or field. The quantity and size of the tomato will change based on what variety you use. Different tomatoes have different amounts of seeds, juice, and pulp. Experiment with what you find in your area.

Serves 4-10.

...continued on next page

Mustard Sauce

1 cup	honey
1 cup	mustard
1/2 cup	balsamic vinegar
	salt & pepper to taste

1.Mix ingredients until well combined.

2.Drizzle over salad and toss gently until all greens are coated.

Serves 4-8.

Makes approx. 2 cups.

The largest vegetable crop in New Brunswick is potatoes, next comes cabbage, sweet corn, broccoli, peas and beans. Most are produced for McCain Foods since they sell many ready to eat vegetables. Small fruit comes as the next crop value with blueberries being the largest. Other small berries like strawberries, raspberries, blackberries and apples are next in line.

Roasted Sweet Red Pepper Dip

2 lbs.	roasted sweet red peppers* finely minced
1/4 cup	sesame oil
1/4 cup	sesame seeds
2 tbsps.	garlic minced
1 tbsp.	soya sauce
1 tbsp.	worcestershire sauce
1/2 cup	sweet onion finely minced
2 cups	soft goat or feta cheese
	salt & pepper to taste

1. Place the roasted red peppers in a shallow baking dish 9" x 9" in size. Sprinkle with the onion and garlic.
2. Sprinkle with the sesame oil, seeds, soya sauce, worcestershire sauce and salt & pepper.
3. Sprinkle with cheese, bake for 20 minutes on 325°F or until cheese is bubbly and starts to turn golden in colour. Let cool slightly and serve while still warm.

*Roasted red peppers can be found in cans or jars in any grocery or specialty food store today. They have been heat roasted and become very sweet. You can choose to make your own, see recipe page 17.

Suggestions: Serve as a vegetable side dish, tossed over pasta, as a spread for toasted rounds, or dipping vegetables.

Makes approx. 3-4 cups.

Roasted Sweet Red Peppers

2 lbs.	sweet or hot red peppers
1/2 cup	olive oil
	salt & pepper to taste

1. Clean peppers but leave them whole. Place peppers in a cooking dish that can withstand high heat. Slowly drizzle the oil over, making sure to coat all peppers lightly. Add a sprinkle of salt & pepper to taste.
2. Roast on broil until peppers have blackened and look very burnt. This can also be done on the barbecue, an open flame or right on the grill on the highest heat. You may also use a kitchen blow torch or a regular blow torch.
3. Once the outside skin has charred, remove peppers from heat. Place them in a dish and cover with plastic wrap so they can sweat. You may also place them into a plastic bag, but tie it shut.
4. Let peppers sit until cold. Remove plastic and gently peel off the blackened skin. This skin should remove very easily at this point. Discard blackened skins and you are left with sweet roasted peppers you can use in any dish. Some blackened skin bits will remain which adds a smoky flair to your peppers.

Makes approx. 4 cups.

Summer Greens and Bacon Sauté

1/4 lb.	bacon or pancetta*
1 tbsp.	lemon juice
1 tbsp.	lemon zest
2 lbs.	greens**
1 tsp.	clarified butter recipe (page 69)
1/2 cup	onion minced
	salt & pepper to taste

1.Fry bacon until crispy, reserve 1 tbsp. of the grease.

2.Pat bacon dry, crumble it and set aside.

3.Add butter and reserved bacon grease to a stainless steel frying pan and fry greens until two thirds cooked. Add lemon juice, lemon zest, onion, and fry until greens start to turn golden on the edges. Serve piping hot.

*Pancetta: Is Italian bacon that has been cured in salt and spices and then air-dried. Found in many delicatessens today.

**Greens – use any greens available such as spinach, asparagus, fiddleheads or brussel sprouts. If using brussel sprouts you may need to par boil them first if they are tough or large in size.

Serves 4-8.

Sweet Crunchy Salad

2 cups	red cabbage
1 cup	fresh cranberries
1/2 cup	pecans
1/2 cup	walnuts
1/2 cup	red onion
1 cup	Granny Smith apple
1 tbsp.	worcestershire sauce
1 tbsp.	soya sauce
1/4 cup	olive oil
1/4 cup	honey
1/4 cup	mustard
	salt & pepper to taste

1. Grate cabbage, apple and onion into a deep mixing bowl.
2. Cut cranberries in half and add to salad and set aside.
3. In a small deep bowl mix the soya sauce, worcestershire sauce, mustard, olive oil, and honey. Stir until mixture is smooth and even.
4. Place both nuts in the salad mixture. Add sauce and restir until all is coated.

Serves 4-8.

Makes approx. 4 cups.

Summer Corn Salsa

6	ears of corn, roasted on the barbecue until slightly blackened
2	red peppers roasted on barbecue until almost completely blackened
1 cup	onion minced
1/2 cup	green onion sliced
1 tbsp.	fresh parsley
1 cup	zucchini diced small
2 tbsps.	lemon juice
1 tbsp.	olive oil
	salt & pepper to taste

1. Make sure when you cook your corn and red peppers on the barbecue that you cook them over very high heat. The corn will take about 5 to 10 minutes until it starts to blacken. The red peppers may take longer so start them first. Once you have charred the red peppers place them in a bowl and cover it with some plastic wrap. Set aside so they can cool and sweat.

2. Continue cooking the corn, then remove from heat. Let cool and slice corn off the cob.

3. When red peppers have cooled, peel off the blackened skin and discard it, it should remove very easily at this point. Chop peppers into 1/4 inch dice. Mix juice, remaining from the peppers, with the olive oil and lemon juice in the last step.

4. Make sure all vegetables are cut up in small dice about 1/4 inch. Place the corn, red peppers, onions, parsley, and zucchini into a deep salad bowl.

5. Mix olive oil, and lemon juice until even. Pour over vegetables and mix well.

Serves 4-8. Makes approx. 3 cups.

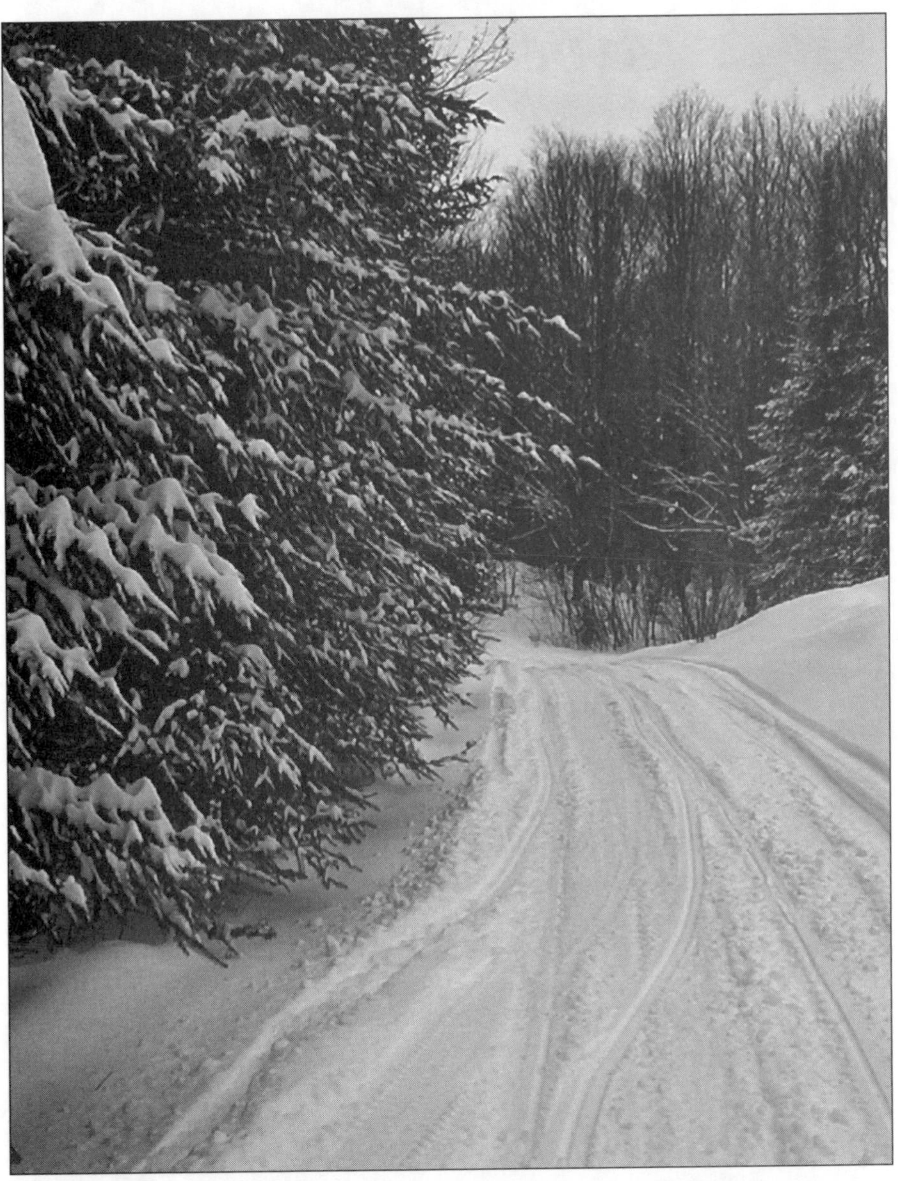

During the cold winter months, you can try one of the many snowmobile trails through New Brunswick's Alpine forests and across rivers of ice. The snow capped peaks and riverside snowscapes reveal the beauty of winter for any outdoorsman. Check for local snowmobile festivals and winter carnival activities in the months of January and February. After a day of pure northern adventure, come inside for a bowl of soup served with crusty bread that will warm you to the tip of your toes.

Avocado Salsa

2 cups	avocado cut into small cubes
1 tbsp. ea.	lemon juice, lime juice
1 tsp.	basil powder
1 tbsp.	coriander powder
1 tsp.	cumin powder
1 cup	sweet onion finely minced (red, vidalia or white)
1 cup	fleshy seeded tomatoes finely diced
1 tbsp.	honey
1 tbsp.	parsley minced
2 tbsps.	balsamic vinegar
1 tbsp. ea.	soya sauce, worcestershire sauce
	salt & pepper to taste

1. Mix all in a bowl until well combined and evenly coated. Let mixture sit covered in the fridge for two hours to allow the flavours to develop. May be used right away as well.

Suggestions: Serve with spicy food, over meat, chicken, fish, or as a savoury fruit dessert with cream.

Serves 4-8. Makes approx. 3 cups.

Avocado Salsa Cold Soup a.k.a. Gazpacho

one	recipe avocado salsa (above)
8 cups	tomato juice
1 cup	tomato paste
	salt & pepper to taste

1. Place all ingredients into a large bowl. Stir well and serve cold on a hot day with crusty bread.

Suggestions: For variations use flavoured tomato juice products, like V8 Juice or Clamato Juice. This may be served hot as a soup as well with some large crunchy croutons on top. Try using for those cool summer night parties in place of your normal vegetable cocktail in your Caesar.

Serves 4-10.

Crunchy Fiddlehead Toast Rounds

1 lb.	fiddleheads
1/4 cup	butter
1 loaf	baguette bread
1 tsp.	garlic minced
1/2 cup	onion minced
	salt & pepper to taste

1. Clean fiddleheads well. Set aside.
2. Slice baguette into rounds and brush with half of the butter. Place on a cookie sheet.
3. In a frying pan, melt the remaining half of the butter.
4. Fry garlic and onion over medium heat until golden brown and caramelized.
5. Add fiddleheads, cook for 3 to 5 minutes until tender.
6. Broil bread rounds until golden brown.
7. Spoon fiddlehead mixture over each bread round and serve immediately.

Serves 4-10.

Garlic Mashed Potatoes

5 lbs.	red or yellow skinned potatoes cooked and mashed
2	whole head bulbs of garlic minced
1/2 tsp.	white sugar
1/4 cup	onion minced
1 tsp.	clarified butter recipe (page 69)
1/2 cup	sour cream
1/2 cup	whipping cream
1/4 cup	butter
	salt & pepper to taste

1. Sauté garlic and onion until golden in clarified butter over medium heat stirring often. Set aside.
2. Boil potatoes until fork tender.
3. Drain off water. Mash well.
4. Add everything else including the sautéed vegetables and then whip with mixer for 3 minutes.

Serves 4-10.

Potatoes are the world's oldest known vegetable. NB farmers have been growing potatoes for over 100 years. They are sold domestically and exported to many other places in the world. Approximately 50 % of the province's potato crops are used as processing potatoes, with the rest being divided for use between table and seed potatoes. We currently export to approx. 35 countries in the world. The earliest record of potatoes being sold in NB dates back to the 17th century.

Sun Dried Tomato Bruschetta

1 cup	sun dried tomatoes soaked in oil
1/4 cup	olive oil
1/2 cup	onion finely minced
1 tbsp.	garlic finely minced
1/2 tsp.	basil powder
1/4 tsp.	oregano flakes rubbed
	salt & pepper to taste

1. Heat tomatoes in oil in microwave for 5 minutes on high heat.
2. Let stand to soften for 5 minutes.
3. Finely mince the sun dried tomatoes.
4. Add remaining ingredients and stir well.
5. Let mixture sit covered for 2 hours at room temperature to allow flavours to develop.

Suggestions: Serve as a salsa, dip or use as a cooking sauce. Use in the classic method of serving on toasted rounds of crusty bread.

Makes approx. 1 ½ cups.

Creamy Fiddlehead and Cheese Casserole

1 recipe	thin béchamel sauce (page 91)
1	lemon rind zested
1/2 cup	lemon juice
3 lbs.	fiddleheads
1/4 cup	parmesan cheese grated
1/4 cup	mozzarella cheese grated
1 cup	dry bread crumbs
1 tbsp.	worcestershire sauce
1 tbsp.	soya sauce
	salt & pepper to taste

1. Clean fiddleheads well and place in a shallow baking dish. Set aside.
2. Make béchamel sauce as per recipe instructions. Remove from heat.
3. To the béchamel sauce add, the lemon juice, zest, cheeses, worcestershire, soya sauce, salt and pepper. Stir well until evenly distributed.
4. Pour sauce over fiddleheads.
5. Sprinkle bread crumbs over top.
6. Bake until bubbly and golden at 325°F.

Serves 6-10.

Tomatoes are another large industry in New Brunswick. In summer hot houses and farmers' fields are plump with flecks of red and green juicy specimens of tomatoes. From tart to sweet to juicy to meaty; from beefsteak to cherry to heirloom varieties, the bounty is endless. Tomato plants thrive well in NB's climate and soil with harvest time being mid to late summer.

Roasted Garlic

6 bulbs	garlic whole
1/2 cup	olive oil
	salt & pepper to taste

1. Slice off 1/2 inch of the top of the bulb exposing the middle making sure to cut as flat as possible so your bulb, when sitting, does not lean to one side.
2. Place cut bulbs and their tops in a shallow 8" x 8" baking dish.
3. Slowly drizzle olive oil over making sure all parts are covered in oil.
4. Sprinkle with salt and pepper.
5. Cover and bake at 300°F for 20 to 45 minutes until the cloves have softened. The cloves will start to look transparent and will start to lift themselves out of the bulb a little.
6. Remove from oven and spread on toasted rounds or use in other recipes. Store in fridge, covered for 2 weeks. Use any oil remaining for cooking as it will have a full bodied garlic flavour.

Serves 4-8.

Sweet Roasted Garlic

1 recipe	Roasted Garlic (above)
1/2 cup	brown sugar
1/2 cup	butter or margarine

1. Cream butter and sugar in bowl until mixed.
2. Equally divide the butter mixture into 6 portions and place one portion on top of each cut open bulb after you have completed step 4 from above.
3. Continue with step 5 from above. The garlic becomes sweet and caramelized.

Fresh Garden Vegetable Stirfry

1 cup	garden peas
1 cup	asparagus tips
1 cup	carrots sliced
1 cup	mushrooms sliced thinly
1 tsp.	garlic minced
1 cup	red onion diced
1 cup	canned chickpeas drained
2 tbsps.	clarified butter recipe (page 69)
1 tsp.	olive oil
1 tbsp.	lemon juice
1 tbsp.	parsley minced
1 tbsp.	white sugar
1 tbsp.	soya sauce
1 tbsp.	worcestershire sauce

1. In a deep large frying pan melt butter and oil together over low heat.
2. Increase heat to medium high.
3. Add carrots and chickpeas. Stir-fry for 2 minutes, stirring constantly.
4. Add the onion, peas, and mushrooms, and fry for 5 minutes stirring often.
5. Add garlic, sugar, asparagus tips, worcestershire sauce, soya sauce, lemon juice, and parsley. Fry for 3 minutes stirring often.

Suggestions: Serve over a bed of rice or noodles, or as a side dish.

Serves 4-10.

Greek Vegetable and Herb Salad

1 cup	artichoke hearts quartered
1 cup	plum tomatoes diced
1 cup	red or vidalia onion diced
1 cup	kalamata olives thinly sliced
1/2 cup	oregano leaves*
1/2 cup	mint leaves*
1/2 cup	basil leaves*
1 cup	feta cheese crumbled
1 cup	mushrooms sliced
1/2 cup	olive oil
1/2 cup	balsamic vinegar
1 tbsp.	lemon zest
	salt & pepper to taste

1. Gently chop herbs into bite size pieces.
2. In a deep salad bowl, toss the artichokes, tomatoes, onion, olives, oregano, mint, basil, mushrooms and cheese. Set aside.
3. In a bowl mix the oil, vinegar, lemon zest, salt & pepper. Stir well.
4. Pour over salad, toss well and serve.

* Fresh herbs only, dried herbs cannot be substituted.

Suggestions: Serve as a side dish, with pasta or on toasted rounds.

Makes approx. 1 litre.

Spicy Sweet Potato Soup

5 lbs.	sweet potatoes
zest	of 1 lemon
1 tbsp.	gingerroot grated
1/2 cup	lemon juice
1/2 tsp.	hot pepper flakes
2	sweet apples peeled, cored, finely minced
16 cups	chicken stock
1 tbsp.	soya sauce
1 tbsp.	worcestershire sauce
1 cup	evaporated milk
	salt & pepper to taste

1. Peel, wash and cut sweet potatoes into 1 inch cubes.
2. Peel, core and finely mince apples.
3. Boil potatoes in the stock until they are very soft. Drain potatoes reserving all liquid.
4. Add apples.
5. Using a potato masher, mash the potatoes well or mix with a hand held mixer on low speed for 2 to 3 minutes until smooth.
6. Add the milk, and add back in some of the cooking liquid until desired consistency is reached.
7. Add the lemon zest, worcestershire sauce, gingerroot, lemon juice, pepper flakes, soya sauce, salt and pepper.
8. Re-blend for 2 minutes.

Suggestion: Serve with crusty bread or dumplings. Serves 4-8.

Creamy Rosemary Potato Salad

3 lbs.	potatoes* skins on
1 cup	yogurt
1 tbsp.	rosemary rubbed
1 tsp.	lemon juice
1 tbsp.	worcestershire sauce
1/2 tsp.	dill
1/2 cup	clarified butter recipe (page 69)
	salt & pepper to taste

1. Scrub potatoes well.
2. Slice potatoes into wedges.
3. Add the lemon, and worcestershire sauce to the clarified butter. Stir well.
4. Place potatoes skin side down on a cookie sheet, pour butter mixture over. Using your hands, rub potatoes until they are well coated.
5. Sprinkle evenly with herbs and then salt & pepper.
6. Bake at 450°F until crispy and golden.
7. Remove potatoes from oven and place in a deep bowl.
8. While the potatoes are still steaming hot pour the yogurt over and stir well to ensure every potato is coated. Make sure your yogurt is at room temperature or slightly warmer before adding to the hot potatoes. Serve hot.

*Red skinned potatoes, Yukon gold and blue fleshed work well in this recipe.

Serves 4-8.

Fiddlehead Sauté

1 lb.	fiddleheads cleaned
1/4 cup	clarified butter recipe (page 69)
1/2 cup	onion finely minced
1 tbsp.	garlic minced
1 tbsp.	lemon juice
1 tbsp.	white sugar
1 tsp.	paprika
	salt & pepper to taste

1. In a stainless steel* frying pan, heat butter over medium high heat.
2. Fry onion and garlic for 2 minutes.
3. Add fiddleheads and stir well.
4. Sprinkle with salt, pepper, lemon juice, sugar and paprika while stirring constantly.
5. Sauté until fiddleheads are tender. About 3 to 5 minutes.

Serves 4-8.

* Green vegetables may sometimes react in certain types of cooking pans and turn darker or even black. They are still ok to eat but may be bitter to the tastebuds. To prevent this, make sure to cook all green vegetables in stainless steel rather than cast iron or aluminum.

Garden Vegetable Skewers

1 lb.	new red skinned potatoes
1 lb.	new white potatoes
1 lb.	baby red onions
1 lb.	baby white onions
1 lb.	yellow pepper
1 lb.	red pepper
1 lb.	small mushrooms
1 lb.	corn
1 lb.	large peas in pod

...continued on next page

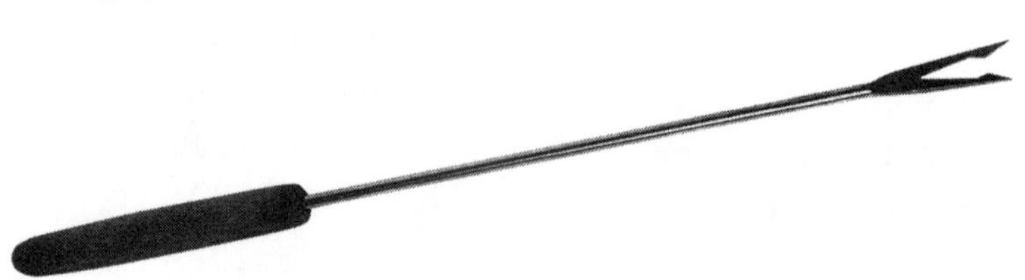

Sweet Basting Sauce

1/2 cup	clarified butter recipe (page 69)
1 tsp.	black pepper
1/2 cup	crushed pineapple
1/2 cup	apple sauce
1 tbsp.	lemon juice
	salt to taste

1. To make sauce, place all the sauce ingredients in a bowl and mix well. Set aside.
2. Clean all vegetables well. Set aside.
3. Parboil potatoes and onion for 5 minutes exactly in salted boiling water.
4. Cool in cold water immediately. Set aside.
5. Peel onions, but leave skin on the potatoes.
6. Cut peppers into 1" pieces.
7. Cut corn into 1" rounds.
8. Arrange vegetables on skewers.
9. Place skewers into a shallow baking dish.
10. Pour basting sauce over and let skewers sit for 10 minutes.
11. Barbecue or bake at 425°F, basting every 5 minutes for 15 minutes.

Serve 4-10.

Creamy Asparagus and Broccoli Bake

1 recipe	thin béchamel sauce (page 91)
zest of	1 whole lemon
1/2 cup	lemon juice
2 lbs.	asparagus
1 lb.	broccoli florets and or stems
1/2 cup	parmesan cheese shredded
1/2 cup	mozzarella cheese shredded
1 cup	dry bread crumbs
1 tbsp.	worcestershire sauce
1 tbsp.	soya sauce
	salt & pepper to taste

1. Clean asparagus and broccoli well.
2. Cut into bite size pieces and layer loosely in a shallow baking dish. Set aside.
3. Make béchamel sauce as per recipe instructions. Remove from heat.
4. To the béchamel sauce add, the lemon juice, zest, cheeses, worcestershire sauce, soya sauce, salt and pepper. Stir well until evenly distributed.
5. Pour sauce over vegetables.
6. Sprinkle breadcrumbs over top.
7. Bake until bubbly and golden brown at 325°F. Approx. 15 to 45 minutes.

Serves 4-10.

Makes 2-3 cups.

Smashed Potatoes

5 lbs.	red or yellow fleshed potatoes quartered
4 liters	chicken stock
1 cup	onion finely minced
1 cup	mushrooms finely minced
1 tsp.	garlic minced
2 tbsps.	clarified butter recipe (page 69) or olive oil
1/2 cup	ranch salad dressing
1/4 cup	sour cream
6	slices of processed cheese
	salt & pepper to taste

1. Sauté onion, mushrooms and garlic in butter, over medium heat stirring often, until golden in color. Set aside.
2. In a large pot bring chicken stock and potatoes to a boil. Cook until potatoes are tender, then mash them well.
3. Add all of the rest of the ingredients including the sautéed vegetables and butter they were fried in. Whip with mixer for 3 minutes.
4. Place into a 9" x 13" casserole dish and broil until top is golden.

Serves 4-8.

Fiddlehead Nut Fry

2 lbs.	fiddleheads cleaned
1 tbsp.	garlic minced
1/4 cup	onion minced
1/4 cup	clarified butter recipe (page 69)
1 tbsp.	soya sauce
1 tbsp.	worcestershire sauce
1 cup	cashews
1 tbsp.	sesame seeds
1 tbsp.	lemon juice
	salt & pepper to taste

1. Place clarified butter in a stainless steel frying pan, increase heat to medium.
2. Wait 1 minute and add all the remaining ingredients.
3. Turn heat back to low and stir until onions are tender.

Suggestion: Serve as a side dish, tossed with pasta, or rice; or on toasted rounds of bread.

Serves 4-8.

Makes approx. 3 cups.

Linguine Tossed with Summer Fresh Garden Vegetables

1 cup	zucchini julienned with peel on
1/2 cup	snow peas julienned
1	red pepper julienned
1 cup	garden carrots julienned
1/2 cup	green onion diced
1 cup	firm, plum tomatoes diced
1 tbsp.	clarified butter recipe (page 69)
1 tbsp.	garlic minced
1 tbsp.	worcestershire sauce
1 tbsp.	soya sauce
1 tsp.	oregano flakes rubbed
1 tsp.	basil flakes rubbed
1 tsp.	white sugar
450g	linguine
	salt & pepper to taste

1. Prepare pasta according to package directions.

2. Sauté all of the vegetables in butter until tender over high heat for 3 to 5 min.

3. Add garlic, soya sauce, worcestershire sauce, oregano, basil, sugar, salt & pepper.

4. Continue to cook and stir gently until heated through.

5. Pour a serving of vegetables over the pasta.

Serves 4-8.

Summer Picnic Coleslaw

1 tbsp.	soya sauce
1 tbsp.	worcestershire sauce
1/2 cup	mayonnaise
2 tbsps.	sour cream
1/2 cup	plain yogurt
2 tbsps.	vinegar
1 tbsp.	oil
1 tbsp.	white sugar
4	broccoli stems peeled and grated
2 cups	carrots grated
2 cups	green cabbage grated
1/4 cup	onion grated
1/4 cup	celery grated
	salt & pepper to taste

1. Mix the first eight ingredients in a large bowl mixing well.
2. Add all the vegetables and toss until all vegetables are coated. Refrigerate for two hours to blend flavours.

Makes 5 cups approx.

Serves 6-12.

Herbed Corn on the Cob

1 cup	butter at room temperature (not melted)
2 tbsps.	parsley
1 tbsp.	chives
1 tsp.	thyme
1/2 tsp.	salt
1/4 tsp.	cayenne powder
1 tsp.	black pepper
1/2 tsp.	garlic powder
1 tbsp.	white sugar
1 dozen	ears of corn

1. Mix all ingredients, except corn, in a bowl until evenly distributed.
2. Wash and prepare corn.
3. Using pastry brush spread a thin layer of butter mixture over every ear of corn and place corn in a shallow baking dish.
4. Wrap each ear snugly in tinfoil for the grill or oven, or parchment paper for the microwave.
5. Cook at 450°F for 15 minutes.

Serves 4-8.

Chapter One

No Cook Pickles

3 lbs.	cucumbers, sliced as desired (thin, thick, peel on or off)
1 cup	onion rounds sliced thinly
2 to 4 cups	white vinegar
2 tsps.	salt
1/2 tsp.	pepper
2 tbsps.	white sugar
2 tbsps.	dill plus sprigs for decoration
1 tsp.	garlic minced
1/2 tsp.	mustard seeds

1. Wash cucumbers well, cut into desired shape and sprinkle with salt in a bowl. Let sit for 30 minutes and then drain off salt water, reserving the water.
2. Mix everything else in a bowl and then add the cucumbers.
3. Stir to distribute evenly and then taste mixture for salt content. Add salt water from cucumbers until desired taste of liquid is achieved.
4. In each bottle add the cucumbers, then fill the rest of the jar with 2/3 pure vinegar and 1/3 reserved pickle water. Add any seasonings like dill seed, dill weed, flakes, mustard seeds etc. Cap bottles. Refrigerate for 24 hours before use for flavours to develop.

Makes approx. 4 cups.

Pineapple Vegetable Salsa

1 cup	sweet green peas (pods removed)
1 cup	red pepper diced
1 cup	yellow pepper diced
1 cup	onion diced
1/2 cup	crushed pineapple
1/2 cup	whole pineapple chunks
1 tbsp.	soya sauce
1 tbsp.	worcestershire sauce
1	dash of dill
	salt & pepper to taste

1. Cut all ingredients into 1/2 inch dice, leaving peas whole.

2. Toss everything into a deep bowl, mix well and serve.

Makes approx 4 cups.

Springtime Fiddlehead Dip 'n Dunk

2 lbs.	fiddleheads
1 cup	apple juice
1 tbsp.	soya sauce
1 tbsp.	worcestershire sauce
1/2 cup	sour cream
1 tsp.	white pepper
1/4 cup	mayonnaise
1 cup	yogurt
1/2 tsp.	garlic minced
1 tsp.	white sugar
1/2 cup	onion finely minced
1 tbsp.	lemon juice
1 tsp.	dill
	salt & pepper to taste

1. Clean fiddleheads well, steam with apple juice until fork tender.
2. Cool immediately in cold water bath to retain their color. Strain well.
3. Finely mince fiddleheads. Place in a deep bowl.
4. Add onion, soya sauce, worcestershire sauce, sugar, garlic, lemon juice, dill, salt & pepper. Mix for a few minutes until sugar is absorbed.
5. Add yogurt, sour cream, and mayonnaise; stir well until evenly mixed.

Suggestion: Serve hot or cold as a dip, with chips and vegetables or serve over pasta. It is sure to be a hit.

Makes 2-3 cups approx.

Christmas Cranberry Baked Beans

8 cups	of ready to serve canned beans in tomato sauce (approx. 3 large cans)
1 cup	cranberries*
1 tsp.	butter
1 tbsp.	garlic minced
1 cup	onion finely minced
1 tbsp.	soya sauce
1 tbsp.	worcestershire sauce
1/2 cup	light brown sugar
1 tbsp.	mustard
	salt & pepper to taste

1. Melt butter in a deep pot over medium to high heat.
2. Add onion and garlic, fry for 3 to 5 minutes until soft.
3. Reduce heat to low and add everything else.
4. Stir well so all ingredients are evenly mixed.
5. Simmer on low heat for 15 minutes.

*Fruit: Can be freshly mashed; jam, jelly, or frozen (thaw first). For a variation try blueberry, raspberry, strawberry, apple, or blackberry.

Suggestion: Serve with biscuits, bread, pastry or Dough Boys stewed in with the beans during the last 10 minutes of cooking. See Dough Boys recipe page 70.

Serves 4-6.

Sautéed Spring Vegetables

1 cup	asparagus cut in 1 inch pieces
2 cups	baby spinach
2 cups	fiddleheads cut into 1 inch pieces
1 cup	sugar snap peas or large sweet peas
1 cup	pecans
2 tbsps.	butter for frying
2 tbsps.	light brown sugar
1/2 cup	onion finely minced
	salt & pepper to taste

1. Melt butter in a frying pan over medium heat. Fry onion for 2 minutes, then add pecans, and fry for 1 more minute. Remove from pan and set aside.
2. In the same pan add asparagus, fiddleheads, sugar and peas. Fry until they are three quarters cooked, about 3 to 5 minutes over medium to high heat.
3. Add spinach and cook until it starts to wilt. Return the onion and pecans to the pan. Fry for 3 minutes more.

Note: Do not use aluminum or cast iron, as this will darken and grey the greens. Use stainless steel, ceramic or glass pots only.

Serves 4-6.

Cleaning asparagus: *all you need to do is run it under cold water to remove any dirt. Scan each stem for bad spots and remove if necessary. To determine where to cut off each stem to avoid the woody, stringy tough husk, hold the stem with both hands, with one hand at the very end of the stem and your other hand about halfway down the stem. Try to break off the root end, and the stem will automatically break where the tough root starts. Discard that piece and devour the rest of the stem. Some thick stems may need to be peeled as they have too thick of a skin. Use a carrot peeler and lightly peel off the thick outer root husk. They need 3 to 10 minutes of cooking varying on method and heat source. They cook fast so always cook just before serving. They are delicious and sweet no matter what method is used. Serve by themselves or with a sauce. Try them baked, broiled, barbecued, fried, grilled, sautéed, boiled, steamed, microwaved, the possibilities are endless. Serve with a creamy cheese sauce, freshly squeezed lemon juice, hot butter or hollandaise sauce, mmmmmm.*

Four Bean Vegetable Salad

1 cup	canned kidney beans
1 cup	canned lima beans
2 cups	canned chick peas
1 cup	canned white beans
1 cup	onion finely minced (red, white or Vidalia)
1 cup	red peppers, diced small
1 cup	green tomatoes diced
1 cup	cucumbers skin on, diced small
1 cup	zucchini, diced small
1/2 cup	green onion, sliced thinly
1 tsp.	sesame oil
1/2 cup	fresh cilantro leaves, packed tightly and minced
1/4 cup	fresh mint leaves, packed tightly and minced
1 tsp.	lime zest
1 tsp.	lemon zest
1 cup	olive oil
1 tbsp.	worcestershire sauce
1 tbsp.	soya sauce
1 cup	sweet vinegar (red wine or apple cider)
	salt & pepper to taste

1. Clean and cut all vegetables. Place them into a deep bowl.
2. Add all remaining ingredients and toss well until all is coated.
3. Place in fridge covered and let sit for 24 hours before using to allow flavours to develop.

...continued on next page

Variation: Choose any beans you like. If you do not like the beans I have listed, use black beans; yellow wax beans; green beans; sweet peas; diced asparagus; or diced plum tomatoes with pulp removed instead.

Serves 6-10.

People always ask if you are supposed to rinse canned beans and vegetables. My rule of thumb is; try the liquid in the can and a bean or vegetable, if you do not like the liquid it is housed in, rinse it off in cold water before using in your recipe. Canned food products are stored in a variety of liquids like water, seasoned water, salt brine or broth. If you are using your canned beans or vegetables in a recipe that has lots of liquid you may choose to reserve the canned liquid to add to your recipe for added concentration of flavour.

Chapter Two

Extras

...all that other yummy stuff

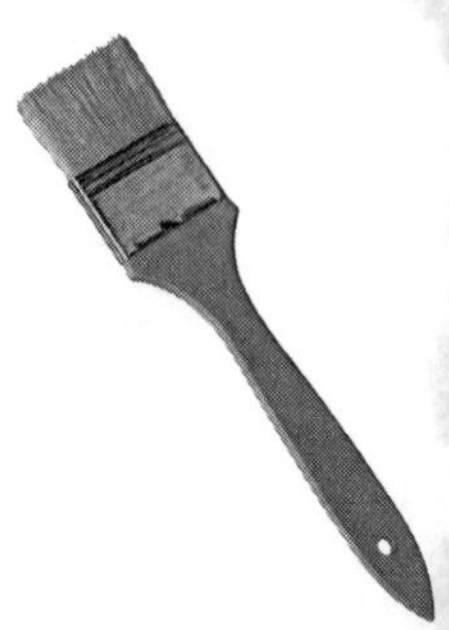

Extras

Apple Salad Vinaigrette

2 cups	applesauce*
1/4 cup	olive oil
1/4 cup	vinegar
1 tsp.	lemon juice
1 tsp.	lime zest
	salt & pepper to taste

1. Purée all ingredients in a food processor or blender for 3 minutes. Strain through a fine sieve.
2. Shake before using. Store in the refrigerator for up to 1 month in a sealed jar.

*Apple – use homemade applesauce for best flavour, you can use jam, jelly, frozen (thaw first), or freshly mashed.

Variations: In place of the applesauce substitute one, or a combination of the following:
Cranberry Vinaigrette - add 2 cups cranberries.
Raspberry Rapture Dressing - add 2 cups raspberries.
Blueberry Blue Sauce - add 2 cups blueberries.
Strawberry Slather - add 2 cups strawberries.
Blackberry Drizzle - add 2 cups blackberries.

Suggestion: Serve as a salad dressing or use as a marinade or condiment for fish, chicken or pork.

Makes 2 cups.

Creamy Blueberry Fruit Dunk

1/2 cup	sour cream
1/2 cup	plain yogurt
2 tbsps.	honey
1 tbsp.	lemon juice
1/4 tsp.	cinnamon
2 cups	fruit*

1. Into a deep bowl, place the fruit. (being jam, jelly, freshly mashed berries or frozen berries thawed)

2. Add all of the remaining ingredients into a deep bowl and stir until evenly mixed.

3. Cool in fridge for 2 hours before using to allow flavours to develop. Restir and serve with seasonal fruit, or vegetables.

*Fruit can be applesauce (homemade), strawberry, raspberry, blueberry, cranberry, blackberry or a combination of the lot.

Variations: In place of the above mentioned fruit use one or a combination of the following:
Red Raspberry Cream Dunk - add 2 cups raspberries.
Creamy Cranberry Sauce - add 2 cups cranberries.
Sweet Strawberry Sauce - add 2 cups strawberries.
Apple Cream Drizzle - add 2 cups applesauce.
Blackberry Dream Cream - add 2 cups blackberries.

Suggestion: Use as a fruit or vegetable dip; as a sauce to bake fruit, chicken, or fish in; or as a dessert topping for pie, dumplings, or cheesecakes.

Makes approx 3-4 cups.

Chapter Two

Bread Crumb Coating

One loaf of bread will usually coat 2 lbs. of meat depending on the fine grind of the crumbs. The bigger the crumbs the more you will need. The finer the crumbs the less you will need and the coating will be crispier.

To make fine crumbs slightly toast the bread. Let cool, and then grate on a cheese grater or use your food processor to make a very fine dust.

Season crumbs with your favourite seasonings like garlic, oregano, Cajun, Mexican, or citrus zests, etc.

You will need to make an egg wash. This will consist of a cream product such as 35%, 18% or 10% cream, yogurt, whole milk, soy milk or buttermilk. (Hint – I find buttermilk works the best). Mix 1 cup cream product with 2 whole eggs, stirring until mixture is smooth, about 2 to 3 minutes by hand.

The next step is to set up an assembly line for coating the food. Start with 3 shallow containers, one for flour, one for egg wash, and one for the crumbs.

Prepare all food items that will require coating, making sure they are dry and not wet to the touch. Dredge the food item through the flour until it is coated. Then dip the item in the egg mixture, the next step is to place the item in the crumb mixture and coat well. Tap off any excess crumbs and place on a baking sheet.

For slow roasted juicy food bake at 325°F or produce a crispy crust in a shorter time at 425°F.

For a healthier lower fat and whole grain coating, use 100% whole wheat bread and flour with a cream product like buttermilk, yogurt, or soy milk. Try melba toast for a very fine crumb that is more suitable for recipes with shorter cooking times.

Lemon Mustard Dressing

1 cup	red wine vinegar
1/2 cup	cider vinegar
1/2 cup	mustard
1/4 cup	lemon juice
1 tsp.	poppy seeds
1 tsp.	minced garlic
1/2 cup	Harvest Time Apple Sauce recipe (page 171)
1 tsp.	lemon zest

1. Blend all together well for 3 minutes and use.

Suggestion: Use as a salad dressing, or marinade.

Makes approx. 2 cups.

Creamy Coconut Rice

2 cups	white basmati or jasmine rice
2 cups	coconut milk
1/2 tsp.	cinnamon*
1 tsp.	cardamom ground*
	salt & pepper to taste

1. Make rice according to package instructions substituting 2 cups of the required liquid for the coconut milk. *Add seasonings if desired.

Suggestions: Try adding 2 tbsps. citrus zest such as lemon, orange, lime or grapefruit for an Asian flair.

Makes approx. 4 cups.

Chapter Two

Thickening

Cornstarch & water method

1. The mixture must be made with cold water as warm water will cook the starch, turning it into glue. You must also add the water to the cornstarch otherwise it will clump. The mixture should be as thick as corn syrup when ready. A large amount would never exceed 3/4 cup of cornstarch powder. For smaller dishes such as a sauce usually 2 to 3 tsps. of cornstarch will do. This method is used for one time meals as it does not reheat well. Once reheated it appears to be jellied and lumpy and will not smooth out completely. Usually because this thickener has a glossy appearance, many cooks prefer it for sauces and stir-fry. You can keep any excess liquid in a sealed jar in the fridge for 3 weeks.

2. Bring the liquid that you want to thicken to a boil and then turn back the heat to just under boiling and add the thickener bit by bit, stirring constantly. The liquid will thicken. If the desired thickness has not occurred, add more thickener. Reduce heat until ready to use.

Flour & water method

1. This mixture has the same properties as the cornstarch mixture. The mixture must be made with cold water, and the water must be added to the flour. First you bring liquid to a boil, reduce it, and then thicken. (same as cornstarch method)

2. For this method you will need at least 1 cup flour to about 2 cups water ratio. Place flour in a tight lidded container, add water and shake well. Open and see if it is too thick or too thin. It should be about as thick as honey. If you use too much it will add a flour taste to the sauce. Bring liquid to a boil, reduce, thicken and stir.

Thickening

Rue method

1. This method is totally different. You melt 1/2 cup of butter on low heat and add flour to it until all the butter is absorbed and the mixture is dry and crumbly, about 3/4 to 1 cup of flour.
2. Remove from heat and let cool, if you want you can store it or you can use it right away if needed. It will store in the fridge for 3 weeks in a sealed jar. It is mainly used for large portions of soups, chowders or clear sauces. You can also use it for smaller amounts like sauces and gravy. Any dish using this method re-heats well.
3. When ready to use, simply add some to whatever you want to thicken and keep stirring, the mixture will dissolve and thicken your dish.

Reducing method

1. Instead of adding a thickener, this method subtracts liquid. You are basically dehydrating a dish when you reduce. If the liquid contains pieces of meat you may want to remove meat so as not to toughen it by the quick high heat.
2. Bring the liquid to a rapid boil on high heat and be careful not to burn it until part of the liquid has evaporated. Typically the liquid is reduced by 1/3. Then return your meat to the dish to reheat it and then toss with the sauce.

Coating food method

1. You can coat food with cornstarch or flour and then brown it in a frying pan with a little oil or butter, then cook your recipe as normal. Then when you add liquid to the dish, the flour/cornstarch will thicken the dish a little.

Garlic Croutons

2 lbs.	bread (1 loaf)
1/2 cup	olive oil
1/2 cup	roasted garlic
1 tsp. ea.	soya sauce, worcestershire sauce
	salt & pepper to taste

1. Mash garlic and add the rest of the ingredients except bread. Stir until smooth.
2. Cut bread into bite sized chunks. Place bread in a bowl and pour oil mixture over it. Stir until bread pieces are well coated.
3. Bake at 350°F until bread is dry and crispy, approx. 15 to 45 minutes stirring every 5 minutes.

Store in fridge for 2 weeks in an airtight container. Makes approx. 1 litre.

Lemon Dill Croutons

1/2 cup	lemon juice
2 lbs.	bread (1 loaf)
1 tbsp.	dill
1/2 cup	olive oil
1 tsp. ea.	soya sauce, worcestershire sauce
	salt & pepper to taste

1. Cut bread into bite size morsels and place in a deep bowl.
2. Mix lemon juice, dill, olive oil, soya sauce, worcestershire sauce, salt & pepper in a bowl until smooth. Pour over bread, stirring until all pieces are coated.
3. Fry over low to medium heat until all bread is crispy stirring often. Approx 10 to 25 minutes.

Creamy Garlic Salad Dressing a.k.a. Caesar Salad Dressing

2 cups	mayonnaise
1 cup	olive oil
2/3 cup	white vinegar
1/4 cup	lemon juice
3 tbsps.	garlic minced or 1 tsp. powder
2 tbsps.	oregano
	salt & pepper to taste

1. Blend all of the ingredients until smooth, about 5 minutes by hand.
2. Let sit overnight before using to allow for the flavour to blend and strengthen.

Note: If you use garlic powder the mixture will last longer and be stronger in flavour as powder is more concentrated.

Suggestion: This is a wonderful creamy dressing for salads, a delicious dipping sauce for vegetables and a great sauce for a meat dish.

Makes approx. one litre. Will keep for 3 weeks refrigerated.

This recipe first appeared in my first cookbook titled: "A Taste of New Brunswick, recipes from our kitchens" August 2001 Neptune Publishing Company Ltd. ISBN: 1-896270-17-4.

Chapter Two

Gravy

Gravy is made from the drippings from meat combined with the cooking liquid from vegetables. Some stock or water may be added to produce the volume of gravy needed. Avoid adding too much liquid to the meat drippings as the flavour will be too diluted. Then the liquid is thickened by various methods.

1. Add spices such as parsley, garlic, mint, basil, soya sauce, or worcestershire sauce to flavour the gravy. For additional flavour, boil 1/2 lb. of meat in 2 cups of water or stock until cooked. Then purée the meat with 1/4 cup onion, and 1/4 cup celery. Add this to the gravy.

2. Commercial gravy browning may be added to darken the gravy. Bring the gravy to a boil, and then turn the heat back so it is just under a boil. Do not add the thickener when liquid is boiling as this will cook the thickener into lumps. Add thickener little by little, stirring constantly until desired thickness is reached. Reduce heat once it starts to thicken.

3. "Au jus" gravy is a thin liquid form of gravy that does not contain the juice from any vegetables. It is only the drippings from the meat that has been reduced by cooking until it thickens naturally. This produces a stronger flavour.

This recipe first appeared in my first cookbook titled: "A Taste of New Brunswick, recipes from our kitchens" August 2001 Neptune Publishing Company Ltd. ISBN: 1-896270-17-4.

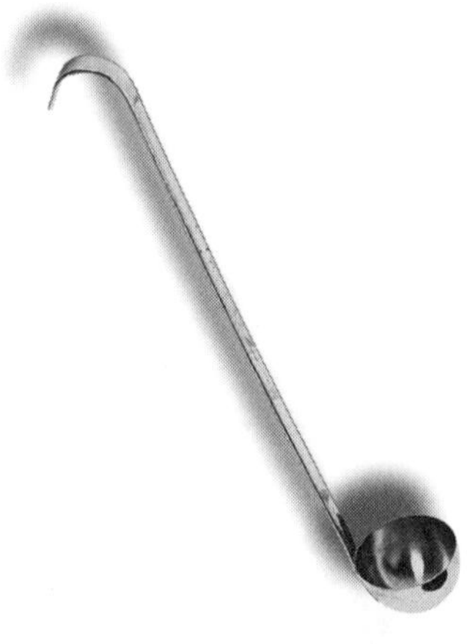

Warm Field Tomato Salad

2 lbs.	tomatoes*
1/4 cup	onion finely minced
1/4 cup	celery finely minced
1 lb.	green beans sliced thinly
1 tbsp.	garlic minced
1/4 cup	olive oil

1. Sauté all in olive oil for 5 minutes over low heat until beans are tender.

* Use fresh garden tomatoes, varieties like yellow, orange, heirloom, cherry, grape, or plum.

Suggestion: Use as a vegetable side dish, or as a base for veggie pizza. Toss with pasta or rice for a full meal.

Serves 4-6.

The crossword game was originally invented by Edward McDonald from Shediac in 1926. It started out like a very prehistoric version of the common scrabble games. Board games and puzzles are a great way to pass the hot summer days sipping punch on the beach or at a BBQ.

Baked Brie

1 cup	Rhubarb Blackberry Chutney recipe (page 63)
1	3" to 5" round wheel of Brie or Camembert cheese

1. Place the whole cheese wheel into a baking dish that has been pre-heated as hot as you can get it.
2. Pre-heat the chutney until it is very hot.
3. Place cheese into the pre-heated baking dish, place heated chutney on top of cheese wheel spreading it out to cover the entire top surface.
4. Cover with plastic wrap or tinfoil for 3 minutes. Serve with toasted bread rounds.

Serves 4-6.

Rhubarb Blackberry Chutney

6 cups	rhubarb thinly sliced
1 cup	blackberries
1 cup	onion finely minced (sweet variety)
1 tsp.	lemon zest
1/2 tsp.	allspice powder
1 tsp.	black pepper
pinch	of salt
1/2 cup	balsamic vinegar*
2	Granny Smith apples peeled, cored and finely minced

1. Clean and prepare all fruit and vegetables.
2. Place all ingredients except the blackberries in a thick bottomed saucepan.
3. Simmer over low to medium heat until rhubarb is soft, approx. 20 to 60 minutes.
4. Add blackberries and bring to a boil. Reduce heat immediately and simmer for 5 minutes.

Suggestion: Serve warm or cold over breakfast items like pancakes and potato latkes. Toss a spoonful over your favourite meat or vegetable.

Makes approx. 4 cups.

Ginger Lime Sauce

1/2 cup	gingerroot grated
1 cup	lime juice
zest	of 1 lime
zest	of 1 lemon
1 tbsp.	olive oil
1 tsp.	garlic minced
1/4 cup	lemon juice
1/2 cup	cilantro leaves packed tightly and minced
1/4 cup	parsley leaves packed tightly and minced
1/4 cup	green onion sliced
	salt & pepper to taste

1. Blend all and let sit for two hours at room temperature to allow flavour to develop.

Suggestion: Use as a marinade, dipping sauce or as a salad dressing.

Makes approx. 2 cups.

Classic Barbecue Sauce

1/2 cup	cider vinegar
1/2 cup	brown sugar
1/2 cup	ketchup
1/4 cup	chili sauce
1/4 cup	worcestershire sauce
1/4 cup	onion minced
1/4 cup	celery minced
1 tbsp.	lemon juice
1/2 tsp.	dry mustard powder
1 tbsp.	garlic minced
1 tsp.	cayenne powder
	salt & pepper to taste

1. Mix all well in a deep saucepan and cook over medium heat stirring often for 15 minutes.

2. Reduce heat to lowest setting and simmer for 15 minutes more.

Makes approx. 2 to 2 1/2 cups.

Tangy 'n Tart Tartar Sauce

2 cups	thick sour cream
1 tbsp.	dill
1 tbsp.	lemon zest
1 tbsp.	lime zest
pinch	of salt
1/4 tsp.	garlic minced
1/2 tsp.	black pepper
1/2 cup	capers minced
1/2 cup	green onion minced
1/2 cup	sweet pickles minced
1/2 cup	cucumbers skin on, minced

1. Blend all ingredients in a glass bowl and let sit covered in fridge for 24 hours for flavours to develop.

Variation: Add 1/4 cup fruit purée like raspberry, blueberry, strawberry etc.

Makes approx. 3 cups.

Note: If you cannot find thick sour cream at your local store you can make your own. Place regular sour cream in a sieve to allow some of the water to drip out. Use double the amount you need as there will be a lot of water that will come out. Hang the sour cream in a cloth to drip or place the cloth inside a sieve and then place the cream on top of the cloth. Place sieve inside another bowl to catch the water. Place cream in fridge to drip for 24 hours.

Lemon Thyme Chicken Bake

2 lbs.	chicken, bone in
4	lemons sliced round
2 cups	onion sliced round and thin (red or vidalia)
1/4 cup	thyme leaves
1 tbsp.	sesame oil
1 cup	chicken stock
1/4 cup	lemon juice
1 tsp.	dill
1/2 tsp.	mint

1. Place chicken skin side down in a shallow baking dish.
2. Cover with herbs, then onion, and then lemon slices.
3. Pour oil, lemon juice and chicken stock over chicken.
4. Bake at 325°F until chicken is golden brown, about 1 hour.

Serves 4.

Raspberry Balsamic Glaze

2 cups	raspberries
1/2 cup	balsamic vinegar
1 tbsp.	honey
pinch	of salt
1/2 tsp.	black pepper

1. Place all ingredients in a thick bottomed saucepan and simmer over medium heat, stirring often until the raspberries have fallen apart.
2. Remove from heat, let cool. Purée or mash until fairly smooth. Strain through a fine mesh sieve to produce a thick smooth glaze.

Variation: Try using a different fruit or combination of fruits like blueberries, strawberries, cranberries, blackberries, Granny Smith or McIntosh apples.

Suggestion: Use as a condiment, basting sauce, marinade, salad dressing or as a dip.

Makes approx. 1 cup.

Butter and Cream

Butter is a by-product of milk. 20 liters of whole milk is churned until it results in 1 to 2 lbs. of butter. The leftover matter from this method of processing is 18 liters skim and buttermilk combined.

Butter is the richness that comes from milk but it is really the fat of the milk. Buttermilk is the leftover by-product, it is low in fat and is very good for cooking. Skim as we all know has no fat so it is a great left over product.

Commercial buttermilk today is made from skim to 3% milk usually and then thickened naturally through the curing processes.

Butter serves many purposes in the cooking world. It provides a flavour like no other for fresh homemade bread, hot steaming potatoes and vegetables plus much more. It is the essential ingredient for pastry cooks.

Clarified Butter is made when you take butter and place it in a heatproof container and then heat it slowly over low heat until the butter is melted completely. The butter will automatically separate itself into a clear golden liquid and the additives of the butter being milk, salt etc…will fall to the bottom. You must then skim off the golden liquid and discard the rest of the matter. The golden liquid is the clarified butter which contains the full butter flavour you are seeking to add to your dish. The clarified butter also has a higher resistance to heat. It can be kept in the fridge for 1 month sealed in a container. You may use butter or margarine anywhere it calls for clarified butter in this book, but you may risk adding more salt or burning your food and it may not taste as intended.

Cream is better than butter, some cooks say, but each has its own special place in the kitchen for any cook. Cream is high in fat so if you are watching your fat intake you can reduce the fat content in some other part of the recipe and keep the cream or take out the cream altogether. The only milk product not always suitable as a substitute is skim milk as it has no fat. This means it has no binding properties to allow thickening to occur.

The higher the fat content in the cream, the less you will require in your recipe to add flavour, and the quicker your dish will thicken.

Types of Cream: 35% cream is known as whipping cream, 18% is commonly referred to as coffee cream, 10% is called cereal cream.

Chapter Two

Dough Boys or Dumplings

These bread like additions to soups and stews are served as an extra filler in the Saturday night soup pot. They can also take the place of potatoes in a stew.

2 cups	flour
1/2 tsp.	salt
2 tsps.	baking powder
1 tbsp.	white sugar
2 tbsps.	butter or margarine (soft)
1 cup	cold water

1. Sift all dry ingredients well in a large deep bowl.
2. Add butter and rub into flour mixture until all is crumbly.
3. Add enough cold water, about 1/2 to 3/4 cup, to stick dough together roughly so that it is a little wet and not too dry. It should be slightly tacky to your fingers.
4. Drop spoon sized or larger balls of dough into a liquid based dish (e.g. soup or stew) for the final 10 to 15 minutes of cooking time.
5. Cover and let steam on the top of your dish for 10 to 15 minutes.

Serves 4-8.

This is a basic recipe that was also included in my first cookbook titled: "A Taste of New Brunswick, recipes from our kitchens" August 2001 Neptune Publishing Company Ltd. ISBN: 1-896270-17-4.

Acadian Chicken Fricot a.k.a. Fricot à la Poulet

A good homemade stock is the key to this recipe. Fine French flavour via our Acadian culture.

8 cups	chicken broth
1 cup	onion sliced round
2 cups	cabbage roughly chopped into medium size pieces
1 cup	carrots thinly sliced
2 cups	white meat chicken pieces pulled from a roasted chicken*
3 cups	medium chunked potatoes
1/2 cup	mushrooms thinly sliced
1/2 tsp.	summer savoury
1/2 tsp.	oregano
1 tbsp.	soya sauce
1 tbsp.	worcestershire sauce
	salt & pepper to taste

1. Place all into a deep pot , simmer over medium heat until potatoes are tender.

Suggestion: Add some dumplings made with a little summer savoury, sage or chicken poultry seasoning.

* When you cook a roasted chicken dinner for the family on a Sunday, save the frame and pull some white meat off to use for your soup. If desired, roast a chicken just for this recipe which will produce a full bodied soup.

Serves 4-10.

Chapter Two

Onions

There are many varieties of onions and they each have their own distinctive taste and use.

Yellow cooking onions are normally yellow in colour and small to medium in size. They are a general purpose onion with a medium flavour. Not too spicy or too sweet.

Spanish onions are yellow and thick skinned, fairly large in size usually 4 inches and up in diameter and have a spicy hotness.

Chives are thin green hollow shoots of the chive plant, not to be confused with green onions. They produce purple flowers which are edible as well. Very strong in flavour with a kind of earthy and musky but savoury onion flavour.

Green onions are small to medium sized tubes of onions with green tops and white bottoms. They are used in Mexican, Asian, and Chinese cooking frequently. They are mild in flavour, but strong in smell.

Shallots are small oval shaped onions that are best described as a cross between an onion and mild garlic. The skins are thick and are a darker yellow orange than most onions. Their flavour is very unique and treasured by many cooks.

White onions peel very easy as they have a thin papery skin, are great for salads and for eating raw as they are mild and sweet. They come medium to large in size but in summer the baby version is grown for pickling.

Red onions are red and white in colour. They have a tough bright deep purplish skin. Once peeled they are very juicy and do bleed their colour a little. If you wish to remove this colour, soak them in a cold water bath for 20 minutes and then rinse under cold water until water runs clear of any colour. They are sweet but contain a hot onion style bite as well. Great for salads and eating raw. They are medium to large in size and come in a baby version as well.

Vidalia onions are sweet and come in a medium to large size. The skin is very thin and papery. Their colour runs from pale yellow to cream with darker yellow patches. The sweetness of this onion makes it a delicacy. The sweetness has no comparison to anything I have ever tasted. It is great in pickles, chutneys, and salads. French onion soup made with this variety of onion is out of this world.

Leeks are very mild and smooth in taste. They are usually 18 inches to 2-3 feet long being pale green on top and white near the bottom. They taste like a cross between a mild onion, mild garlic and celery for a flavour description. They make great soups and chowders and are perfect on pizza. Commonly used in French cuisine and are often paired with salmon.

Fresh spring onions are giant green onions with medium bulbs on the bottom of long hollow dark green shoots. Very strong and a medium onion bite.

Shop around your local grocery store and farmers' market for many varieties to try.

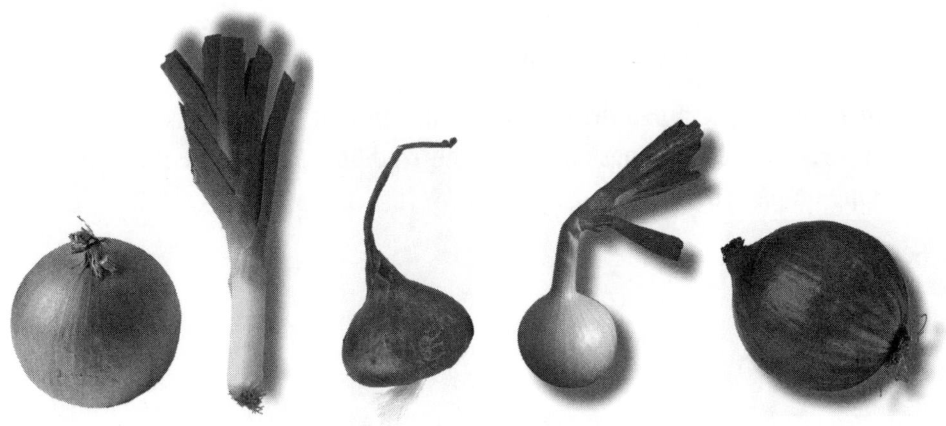

Sunday Supper Roast Beef and Vegetables

5 to 8 lbs.	roast beef, (sirloin, striploin, T-bone)
3 cups	onion cut into medium sized chunks
1 cup	mushrooms halved
12 cups	beef broth
3 cups	water
1 tbsp.	soya sauce
1 tbsp.	worcestershire sauce
1 lb.	baby carrots
3 lbs.	potatoes

1. In a deep large roaster, place roast with 4 cups broth and 2 cups water. Cover.
2. Bake at 300°F for 1 hour without opening oven door.
3. Check roast, turn up heat to 475°F and brown roast all over.
4. Let roast get crispy all over but do not let pan dry out.
5. Add remaining broth, the rest of water, and all other ingredients to the roaster and stir well.
6. Bake at 350°F until vegetables are tender. About 30 minutes to 1.5 hours.

Suggestion: Thicken pan drippings to make gravy if desired or serve stew style. Save some drippings and make the Traditional Yorkshire Pudding recipe on page 81.

Serves 4-8.

Asiago Honey Mustard Sauce

1/2 cup	mustard*
1 litre	cream product**
1 cup	Asiago cheese grated
1 tbsp.	soya sauce
1 tbsp.	worcestershire sauce
	salt & pepper to taste

*Mustards are available in different varieties and forms, try Dijon or grainy for this recipe, but prepared yellow mustard is fine as well.

**Cream product can be one or a combination of the following: coffee cream, whipping cream, yogurt, buttermilk, evaporated milk, cereal cream, soy milk or silken tofu.

1. Cook all ingredients together in a small sauce pan over medium heat until cheese is melted, stirring the entire time.

Suggestion: Serve piping hot or at room temperature. Serve over fish, meat, chicken, or vegetables.

Makes approx. 5 1/2 cups.

Rappie Pie a.k.a. Paté à la Rapture

5 lbs.	starchy* potatoes grated
2 lbs.	chicken with bone in
1 cup	onion chopped
1 cup	carrots chopped
1 cup	celery chopped
2	bay leaves
1/2 lb.	pork fat diced small
8 to 16 cups	broth**
	salt & pepper to taste

1. Bake chicken with onions, carrots, celery and bay leaves until cooked and falling off the bone. Discard bay leaves. Let cool down, remove all bones and non-edible matter and discard. Set meat and vegetables aside in a bowl.
2. Layer 1 cup broth into the bottom of a casserole dish, next place a layer of meat, a layer of potatoes, and repeat until you end up with potatoes on top.
3. Cover the top with the diced cubes of pork fat spaced out as evenly as possible. Bake at 350°F for 30 minutes to 1 to 1 1/2 hours based on the thickness of your pan. The top will be golden brown and the juices from inside will be bubbling up.

Serves 6-12. Makes one 9" x 13" pan.

*The potatoes must be the starchiest variety you can find to produce the best results. These include red skinned, yellow fleshed, Yukon gold, and russets to name a few. Start by grating the raw potatoes into a deep bowl, you will notice they produce a lot of juice which is very starchy. Place the potatoes in a cheesecloth or another cloth bag strong enough to withstand your attempts to remove all liquids. You can mash it with a potato masher, can hang it up to drip, hand squeeze, or squish it with a heavy object over a drain. The goal is to remove as much of the liquid from the grated potatoes as possible. Discard the liquid.

**You will be rehydrating these grated potatoes with a very flavourful broth. The broth must be the best flavour you can produce for this dish to turn out just like grandma used to make. Place the grated and drained potato matter into a deep bowl or pot and slowly add broth until you reach the consistency of thick mashed potatoes, no heat required. You will then layer the potato mixture with meat and or vegetables into a deep casserole dish.

Potatoes are best stored at 7 to 10 degrees Celsius. Keep them in a dark place to prevent sprouting. Remove them from plastic bags if you buy them this way as they will sweat and rot over time. Exposure to light may turn them green and they sometimes become bitter. If you store them too cold they will get grey spots, they are still ok to eat but will discolour as they cook becoming greyer in colour and their taste may change.

The popularity of Rappie Pie increased when women discovered that the water that was squeezed from the potatoes was very high in starch. This liquid filled the need for starch in the laundry room. They then added the broth back into the potatoes and layered the potatoes in deep casserole dishes with mounds of meat and sometimes vegetables. The top was then covered with little cubes of port fat which help form a crispy flavourful crust over top during the baking process and filled the houses with a delicious smell. The meat was often rabbit hence the name, but was soon replaced with any meat on hand; chicken became the favourite in the years soon after its creation. Sometimes it was made with seafood like clams or scallops. It continues to be a popular dish today so you can purchase store-bought grated potatoes specially made for rappie pie. Check with your local grocer.

Creamy Greek Poppy Seed Dressing

1 cup	thick sour cream
1 cup	yogurt*
2 tbsps.	poppy seeds
2 tbsps.	garlic minced
1/4 tsp.	oregano
1/4 tsp.	thyme
1/4 tsp.	basil
1 tbsp.	lemon juice
1 tbsp.	lemon zest
	salt & pepper to taste

1. Mix all into a deep bowl stirring until evenly mixed.

***Variation:** try using a flavoured yogurt like lemon, orange, mint or vanilla for a different taste.

Suggestion: Serve as a dip or as a salad dressing. Use as a mayonnaise.

Makes approx. 2 cups.

Greek Vinaigrette Dressing

1 cup	red wine
1/2 cup	red wine vinegar
1 cup	olive oil
2 tbsps.	minced garlic
1 tbsp.	parsley
1 tbsp.	honey
1/4 cup	red onion finely minced
	salt & pepper to taste

1. Stir all ingredients in a deep bowl until evenly mixed.

Makes approx. 2 cups.

Simple Syrup

1 cup	white sugar
1 cup	water

1. Place both ingredients into a small pot and stir until sugar is dissolved.
2. Bring to a boil over high heat. Boil for 1 minute and remove from heat.
3. Let cool or use syrup right away.

Use in any recipe that calls for a sweetener.

Makes approx. 2 cups.

Syrup will keep in fridge for 2 weeks.

Blue Cheese Dressing

1 cup	blue cheese* crumbled
1 tsp.	black pepper
1 tbsp.	lemon juice
1 tbsp.	lemon zest
1 tbsp.	mustard**
1 tbsp.	olive oil
3 cups	cream***
	salt to taste (optional)

* Blue cheese is salty so make sure you taste it before you add any extra salt.

**Mustard comes in many varieties, try grainy or Dijon.

***Cream – can be buttermilk, yogurt - plain or flavoured, coffee cream, cereal cream, whipping cream, soy milk or silken tofu.

1. Mix all ingredients in a deep bowl or food processor until combined, cheese will stay a little lumpy. (You may purée longer for a smoother texture).

Suggestions: Try adding some freshly minced herbs, like parsley or cilantro for added flavour.

Makes approx. 1 litre.

Will keep in fridge covered for 1 month.

Traditional Yorkshire Pudding

1 cup	flour
1 tsp.	salt
1 cup	milk
2	eggs
1/4 tsp.	garlic powder
1 tbsp.	soya sauce
1 tbsp.	worcestershire sauce
1 cup	meat drippings
	pepper to taste

1. Place all of the ingredients, except meat drippings, in a deep bowl.
2. Mix until smooth and well blended. Place in refrigerator covered.
3. Lightly grease a 9" x 13" baking dish or 24 muffin cups and pour in the meat drippings. Place in a 400° F oven until pan is hot.
4. Remove pan from oven, add Yorkshire mixture to pan. Return to oven for 1/2 hour.

Hint: You can make this mixture the night before and keep it in the fridge overnight. This allows the mixture to bind, thus producing a fluffier bread.

This English recipe is popular in many loyalist NB kitchens; it is from my first cookbook titled: "A Taste of New Brunswick, recipes from our kitchens" August 2001 Neptune Publishing Company Ltd. ISBN : 1-896270-17-4.

Chicken and Greens Soup

8 liters	of the best chicken broth available
4 cups	fresh green vegetables (mixture of fava beans, sugar snap peas, snow peas, asparagus, fiddleheads, garden peas, collard greens, spinach, or string beans)
1 tbsp.	soya sauce
1 tbsp.	worcestershire sauce
1/2 tsp.	dried dill flakes
1 tbsp.	butter
1	bay leaf
1 cup	onion finely minced
1 cup	mushrooms thinly sliced
1/4 cup	white sugar
	salt & pepper to taste

1. In a deep pot, sauté the onion and mushrooms in butter. Add all greens and sauté for 3 minutes on high stirring constantly.
2. Add all remaining ingredients to the pot and bring to a boil.
3. Reduce heat to low. Simmer until greens are tender. Approx. 5 to 10 minutes.

Suggestion: Serve piping hot with a dollop of sour cream in the middle and crusty bread on the side. Try adding some savoury dumplings or rice for a variation.

Note: Use a stainless steel or any non-reactive pan, otherwise the greens may turn grey, blacken or become bitter.

Serves 4-6.

Grilled Maple Glazed Chicken

1 recipe	maple glazed chicken sauce thickened (below)
2 lbs.	chicken pieces of choice

1. Par boil chicken pieces (if they have bone), this reduces the complete cooking time, tenderizes the meat and removes most of the fat content.
2. Transfer chicken pieces to the grili and baste constantly with the maple sauce for the rest of cooking time. Dip whole pieces in sauce and return to grill or bake in the oven at 325° F for 45 minutes to 1 1/2 hours until chicken is cooked, basting often.

Maple Glazed Chicken Sauce

1 cup	maple syrup
2 cups	water
2 tbsps.	garlic minced
1/4 cup	soya sauce
1 tbsp.	butter
	salt & pepper to taste

1. Place all of the ingredients in a pot and stir until well mixed.
2. Bring mixture to a slow boil over medium heat. Remove from heat.
3. Thicken if desired, or pour over meat and bake. (e.g. ribs, chicken, pork, fish etc.). See Thickening recipe instructions on page 56.

Makes approx. 2 cups.

Canadian Cheddar Cheese Sauce

2 tbsps.	butter
2 tbsps.	flour
1/2 tsp.	mustard
1 cup	milk
2 to 3 cups	cheddar cheese grated
	salt & pepper to taste

1. Melt butter with mustard on low heat until evenly mixed.
2. Add flour, the mixture will be lumpy and dry. Stir until all flour is absorbed.
3. Slowly add milk, stirring constantly until all of the flour mixture dissolves and the sauce is smooth.
4. Increase the heat to high, stirring constantly until the sauce begins to thicken.
5. When the desired thickness is achieved, turn off the heat and quickly stir in the cheese, stirring until the cheese is completely melted. Serve immediately. This sauce can be made ahead but it will be a little thinner when reheated.

* Optional flavours to add to finished sauce: worcestershire sauce, soya sauce, fresh herbs, hot peppers or salsa.

Variation: Substitute any cheese flavour you like instead of the cheddar.

Suggestion: Serve this sauce over steamed fresh vegetables or with a fish or chicken dish.

Makes approx. 1 - 1 1/2 cups.

This is a basic recipe that was also included in my first cookbook titled: "A Taste of New Brunswick, recipes from our kitchens" August 2001 Neptune Publishing Company Ltd. ISBN : 1-896270-17-4.

Summer Fruit Salsa

1 cup	mango diced
1 cup	peaches or nectarines diced
1/4 cup	lime juice
1/2 tsp.	lime zest
1/2 cup	lemon juice
1/2 tsp.	lemon zest
1 tbsp.	mint leaves minced
1/4 cup	sweet onion minced
1/4 tsp.	garlic minced
1/4 cup	sugar
1/4 cup	crushed pineapple
1/2 cup	Granny Smith apples finely minced
	salt & pepper to taste

1. Mix all well and place in fridge for 1 hour for flavours to develop.

Suggestion: Serve with cheese, meat, fish or chicken.

Makes 3 cups.

All of these fruits are enjoyed by many nationalities in a variety of ways. Check your local fruit stand for imported high quality exotic fruits to experiment with.

Spicy Blueberry Baked Beans

1/2 cup	green chilies minced
8 cups	ready to use canned beans
1 cup	blueberry jam, jelly or mashed fresh or frozen* berries
1 cup	onion finely minced
1 tbsp.	garlic minced
2 tbsps.	regular mustard
1 cup	light brown sugar
3 tbsps.	soya sauce
3 tbsps.	worcestershire sauce
1 tbsp.	green tabasco sauce
1 tbsp.	butter
	salt & pepper to taste

1. In a deep pot, fry onion and garlic in butter over high heat for 3 minutes.
2. Add chilies, and fry 1 more minute.
3. Place everything else in the pot and simmer for 15 minutes on low.

*If using frozen berries ensure they are thawed before using.

Makes approx. 1 to 1 ½ liters.

Classic Italian Bruschetta

3 lbs.	tomatoes roughly chopped (baby, grape, cherry or plum)
1	whole head garlic minced
1 cup	onion minced
1 tbsp.	oregano flakes rubbed
1 tbsp.	basil flakes rubbed
1 cup	olive oil
1/2 cup	balsamic vinegar
1 to 2	loaves of baguette bread
	salt & pepper to taste

1. Place all ingredients into a 9" x 13" glass casserole dish, except bread.
2. Place roasting pan on a cookie sheet to provide an insulated bottom.
3. Bake at 325°F for 1 hour, stirring a few times during cooking.
4. Serve slightly warm on toasted baguette rounds.

Makes approx. 4 cups.

Will keep in fridge for 2 weeks.

There are many varieties of basil to try, such as genovese, napolitano, sweet, cinnamon, lemon, bush, clove, Thai, licorice, holy, camphor, opal, purple, red, anise, and many more. Basil is a wonderful and popular compliment to tomatoes.

Coq au Vin

3 lbs.	chicken pieces bone in
2 cups	onion minced
3 cups	potatoes large diced
1 cup	mushrooms sliced
1 cup	carrots grated
1 tbsp.	garlic minced
2	bay leaves
1 tsp.	thyme
1 tsp.	parsley
4 slices	bacon diced
1 cup	red wine
1/4 cup	clarified butter recipe (page 69)
1 to 3 liters	chicken stock to cover
	salt & pepper to taste

1. Brown bacon in frying pan, add butter and fry chicken until it has some colour, browning it as much as possible over medium to high heat.

2. Add all remaining ingredients and bake in the oven for 45 minutes to 1 ½ hours at 325°F or until sauce starts to thicken and chicken falls off the bone.

Suggestion: Serve piping hot with bread for dipping or over a bed of mashed potatoes.

Serves 4-8.

Cold Pasta Salad

Salad

6 cups	cooked, cooled, rinsed pasta of choice
1 cup	celery thinly sliced
1 cup	garden tomatoes diced
1/2 cup	carrot grated
1 cup	green pepper finely diced
1 cup	sweet onion finely minced

Salad Dressing

3/4 cup	French style salad dressing
3/4 cup	Italian style salad dressing
1/2 cup	mayonnaise
1/4 cup	white sugar
2 tbsps.	parsley leaves chopped

1. Mix salad dressing in a bowl and set aside.

2. Toss salad ingredients in a deep bowl until evenly distributed.

3. Pour salad dressing over and toss well. Serve cold.

Serves 4-6

Tomato Cheese Melt

2 slices	of bread or flour tortilla
4 round slices	of tomato (very ripe or green tomatoes)
2 tsps.	mayonnaise, ranch salad dressing, or herbed cream cheese
1/4 cup	cheddar cheese* grated
	salt & pepper to taste

1. Spread 1 tsp. of mayonnaise, ranch dressing or herbed cream cheese on each piece of bread.
2. Top one slice of bread with the tomatoes.
3. Sprinkle cheese on top of the tomatoes.
4. Top with other slice of bread.
5. Fry, grill or broil until crispy.

* Use a flavour of cheese you like if cheddar is not your favorite. Swiss, blue, mozzarella, etc…

Makes one sandwich.

Basic White Sauce a.k.a. Béchamel Sauce

Depending on the recipe there are three consistencies of this sauce:

1 cup	milk
2 tbsps.	butter
1 tbsp.	flour (2 tbsps. for medium, 3 tbsps. for thick)
	salt & pepper to taste

Thin: result of sauce is similar to the consistency of evaporated milk
Medium: result of sauce is similar to the consistency of honey
Thick: result of sauce is similar to the consistency of ketchup
Optional: One tbsp. of soya sauce and or worcestershire sauce may be added. This will change the colour of the sauce to beige rather than white.

1. Melt butter over low heat in a small heavy saucepan. Add the flour and stir until it is absorbed. Cook for 2 minutes.
2. Remove from heat.
3. Slowly add cold milk a little at a time, whisking constantly until all flour is dissolved.
4. Once all the flour has been absorbed in the milk, return pot to the heat. Increase the heat to medium stirring constantly until the desired thickness is achieved. Approx. 2 to 10 minutes depending on heat source.

This sauce is a base for any dish requiring a creamy sauce. You may add any seasonings of choice, and then use it right away. You can use the sauce as a base for a casserole, cheese sauce or white gravy; a very versatile sauce base.

Basil Oil

2 cups	fresh basil leaves (packed tightly)
2 cups	olive oil
	salt & pepper to taste

1. Place oil and basil in a food processor and purée for 3 minutes until all leaves are puréed.
2. Strain through cheesecloth or a fine sieve to remove all basil particles. This is not necessary if you like the basil chunks in your dish but they will burn once cooked if using this oil for cooking.
3. Bottle and use. Keeps for 1 month in fridge covered.

Suggestion: Use for salad dressings; as a cooking oil; or anywhere you would use oil.

Variations – in place of the basil add one or a combination of the following:
Mint – 1 cup fresh mint leaves – Greek style dishes, lamb and for desserts.
Ginger – 1 cup fresh gingerroot – Thai style dishes and pork.
Thyme – 1 cup fresh thyme leaves – Greek style, try chicken.
Rosemary – 1 cup fresh leaves – Mediterranean, use for lamb, chicken or pork.

White Bean Stew

1 cup	canned white beans with juice
2 cups	crushed tomatoes
8 cups	stock*
1 tbsp.	basil flakes
1/2 tsp.	oregano flakes
1 tsp.	parsley flakes
1 tsp.	coriander or cilantro flakes
1 cup	mushrooms thinly sliced
1/2 cup	onion minced
1/2 cup	canned water chestnuts, thinly sliced
1 tbsp.	soya sauce
1 tbsp.	worcestershire sauce
1 tbsp.	garlic minced
1 tbsp.	green tabasco sauce
1/2 cup	celery minced
1/2 cup	red pepper minced
1/2 cup	yellow wax beans diced
1/2 cup	green beans diced

1. Place all into a deep pot. Make sure liquid level is 2 inches above ingredients. You may need to add additional water or stock.

2. Simmer over medium heat until vegetables are tender.

*Stock can be water, chicken, beef, vegetable or fish.

Serves 6-12.

Curried Indian Rice

3 cups	white rice cooked and cooled
1/4 cup	clarified butter recipe (page 69)
1/2 cup	onion finely minced
1 tbsp.	garlic finely minced
1 tsp.	gingerroot grated
1 cup	firm plum tomatoes, pulp removed and reserved, diced small
1 tbsp.	curry power
1 tbsp.	worcestershire sauce
2 tbsps.	soya sauce
1/2 cup	lime juice
	salt & pepper to taste

1. Make rice according to package instructions. Cool, fluff with a fork, and set aside.
2. In a large deep frying pan over medium heat, sauté the garlic, onion and gingerroot in the butter for 3 minutes.
3. Add the tomatoes and fry for 2 minutes stirring constantly.
4. Add curry powder, worcestershire sauce, soya sauce, and lime juice. Cook for 2 more minutes.
5. Reduce heat to low, add rice to mixture, and stir until rice is coated well and heated through.

Suggestion: You may add the reserved tomato pulp to step 3 if you like or strain it first to remove any seeds.

Serves 4-8.

Cranberry Yorkshire Pots

1 recipe	Traditional Yorkshire Pudding recipe (page 81)
1 cup	crushed fresh cranberries, jelly or jam
1/4 tsp.	cinnamon

1. Prepare Traditional Yorkshire Pudding according to instructions and then place into muffin tins.
2. In a bowl, mix the cranberries and cinnamon together.
3. Place one heaping tablespoon of cranberry cinnamon mixture in the center of the top of each uncooked muffin and place into the oven to bake.
4. Bake according to Traditional Yorkshire Pudding recipe.

Suggestion: goes great with chicken, turkey, pork, lamb, ham and beef.

Serves 6-12.

Maple Breakfast Tart

1 cup	Harvest Time Applesauce recipe (page 171)
2 lbs.	bacon
1/2 cup	maple syrup
1 recipe	Perfect Pie Crust, single layer only (page 193)
1 recipe	Crumble Mixture (page 172)

1. Fry bacon until it is three quarters cooked.
2. Drain fat and crumble bacon into small pieces.
3. Place a single pie shell into a well-greased pie pan.
4. Spread applesauce, then bacon bits, and then maple syrup over the pie crust.
5. Sprinkle crumble mixture on top of pie.
6. Bake at 425°F until golden.

Suggestion: Serve with a wedge of cheddar cheese or drizzle cheese sauce over top; add a side dish of fluffy scrambled eggs.

Serves 4-10.

Maple sugar shacks dot the winter wonderlands of New Brunswick. Take a tour, pour some sap, collect it, cook it, and take home some sugar pie, or freshly made snow candy.

Apple Walnut Wild Rice

1 cup	Granny Smith or Macintosh apple minced
1 cup	wild rice, cooked and cooled
2 cups	white long grain rice cooked and cooled
1/2 cup	sweet onion finely minced
1 cup	mushrooms thinly sliced
1/4 cup	green onion finely chopped
1/2 cup	walnut pieces roasted*
2 tbsps.	butter
1/4 cup	soya sauce
1 tbsp.	worcestershire sauce
	salt & pepper to taste

1. In a deep bowl, mix the white and wild rice until evenly distributed. Toss in the green onion and mix again. Set aside.
2. In a frying pan over medium heat, melt the butter. Fry the sweet onions for 3 minutes.
3. Add mushrooms, stirring constantly. Fry until the mushrooms are golden brown about 8 to 12 minutes.
4. Add everything else except for the rice and fry for 2 more minutes.
5. Add rice and keep stirring until rice is hot enough to serve.

*To roast walnuts, place the raw nuts on a cookie sheet and put into the oven for 5 to 10 minutes on 350°F or until you can smell the nuts. Remove from oven, salt if desired and let cool.

Suggestion: You can also serve this as a room temperature rice salad.

Serves 4-10. Makes approx. 5 cups.

Tortiére Pie

1 double layer	Savoury Pie Crust recipe (page 194)
2 lbs.	pork, dark meat
1 cup	onion minced
1 tsp.	garlic minced
1 tbsp.	worcestershire sauce
1 tbsp.	soya sauce
1/2 tsp.	gingerroot grated or 1/4 tsp. powder
1/2 tsp.	rosemary rubbed
1/2 cup	mashed potatoes
1 cup	mushrooms sliced
2 cups	beef broth
1 tbsp.	cornstarch
	salt & pepper to taste

1. Lightly sprinkle oil in a shallow frying pan, and set stove to medium to high heat. Fry pork until it is well browned and caramelized. The meat should look almost burnt with residue stuck to the bottom of the pan.
2. Reduce heat to low, remove meat and set aside.
3. Fry onion in same pan for a few minutes loosening the brown bits on the pan.
4. Add garlic, gingerroot, mushrooms, rosemary, and then fry for 5 minutes until mushrooms are cooked.
5. Add broth, worcestershire sauce and soya sauce and return meat to pan. Cover tightly, and simmer over low heat until meat falls apart easily, adding more broth or water as needed. Meat must not dry out and you must end up with at least 2 cups finished broth. Approx. 30 minutes to 2 hours of cooking.

...continued on next page

6. Cool mixture and pull meat apart into strings or small bite size pieces. Discard any fat, gristle and bones.
7. Place the bottom pie shell in pie pan and then pour in meat mixture and broth.
8. Sprinkle cornstarch evenly over meat mixture.
9. Thinly spread the entire pie with a layer of mashed potatoes.
10. Add top pie crust.
11. Pierce a few vent holes and bake at 375°F until crust is golden and juices bubbly.

Makes one 9 inch pie.

Mustard Tarragon Glaze

1 cup	sour cream
1/2 cup	plain yogurt
1/2 cup	honey mustard
1/2 cup	whole grain mustard
1/4 cup	regular mustard
1 tbsp.	lemon juice
1 tbsp.	lime juice
2 tbsps.	tarragon flakes or 1 tsp. dried
	salt & pepper to taste

1. Mix all well in a bowl. Let sit for 1 hour in fridge to allow the flavours to develop.

Suggestion: Use as a sauce for dipping, baking or basting.

Makes approx. 3 cups.

Strawberry Chicken Roast

4	chicken pieces, bone in (approx. 2 lbs.)
1 cup	chicken stock
1 tbsp.	worcestershire sauce
1 tbsp.	soya sauce
1 tbsp.	hot sauce
1 cup	strawberries freshly mashed
1/4 tsp.	nutmeg
1 tsp.	rosemary rubbed
1	lemon sliced round
1 tsp.	butter
	oil for frying
	salt & pepper to taste

1. Place chicken pieces in a hot frying pan with some oil on high heat to brown each piece on all sides. Drain chicken pieces and place in baking dish. Set aside.
2. Place the strawberries in a mixing bowl, and mash them well.
3. To the strawberries, add the worcestershire sauce, soya sauce, hot sauce, stock, nutmeg, rosemary, salt & pepper and mix well.
4. Pour over chicken, ensuring sauce is evenly distributed over chicken. Layer the lemon slices over top of the sauce. Cover with tinfoil.
5. Bake at 350°F for 30 minutes. Check to ensure liquid has not dried out. Lightly stir dish. Cook for another 30 minutes and serve.

Suggestion: You may drain off all fruit and purée it for a nice sauce to accompany your dish. The meat will turn pink from the colour of the strawberries. To ensure food is cooked you should use a meat thermometer in the thickest part of the chicken to ensure it has reached a correct and safe temperature of 165°F to 180°F.

Serves 4.

Sweet Summer Strawberry Gravy

4 liters	of your favourite gravy (chicken, pork or beef)
1 cup	of fruit*

1. Add fruit to gravy and stir well, heat and serve.

Suggestion: For the more daring cooks out there try more than one fruit at a time. All of them go great over any vegetable dish.

Variations:

Tart 'n Tangy Cranberry Gravy - great over any chicken dish.
Summer Blueberry Gravy - great over pork and with red wine.
Red Raspberry Gravy - delicious on fish and pork.
Harvest Hearty Apple Gravy - on pork it's great, lamb even better.
Blue Blackberry Gravy - great on pork, and any game.

Makes approx. 4 liters.

Savoury Dry Stuffing

6 cups	dry bread
1/2 cup	meat drippings with fat (chicken, beef, turkey etc.)
1 cup	onion medium diced
1 cup	carrots grated
1/2 cup	mushrooms sliced
1/2 cup	celery medium diced
1/2 cup	butter melted
1/4 cup	chicken poultry seasoning
1 tbsp.	sage
1 tbsp.	worcestershire sauce
	salt & pepper to taste
	Any other seasonings of choice

1. Break bread into 1/2 inch to 1 inch cubes. Place in a large deep casserole dish that has been lightly greased.
2. Add all vegetables and stir well to distribute evenly. Set aside.
3. In another bowl, mix the butter, worcestershire sauce, salt, pepper, sage, poultry seasoning and drippings until combined. Pour over bread pieces and toss well.
4. Bake at 325°F until golden and crunchy, tossing every 20–30 minutes. This may take 1 to 3 hours depending on bread type and oven.

Suggestion: Serve with poultry or any meat any time of the year, not just at Christmas. Makes a great addition to the top of a hot steaming bowl of homemade chicken soup or even use as croutons.

Makes approx. 6 cups.

Chapter Three

Seafood

The catch of the day…salty or fresh!

…continued on next page

SEAFOOD

Chapter Three

Seafood

The catch of the day...salty or fresh!

Blackened Salmon

2 tbsps.	cumin powder
2 tbsps.	coriander powder
1 tbsp.	black pepper
1 tsp.	salt
1 tsp.	crushed chilies
2 lbs.	salmon
1/4 cup	olive oil
1	whole lemon cut into wedges
zest	of 1 lemon

1. Mix cumin, coriander, pepper, salt, chilies and zest in food processor or food grinder until it is like dust.
2. Place salmon whole or cut up onto a parchment paper lined cookie sheet. Brush with oil.
3. Dust each piece of salmon with the spice mixture until coated well.
4. Broil in oven or on grill until salmon is blackened, approx. 10 to 25 minutes. Do not turn fish over. Remove from oven and let salmon sit for 5 minutes. Squeeze lemon juice over top and serve.

Serves 4.

Hot Thai Shrimp

2 lbs.	shrimp in the shell
1/2 cup	jalapeno peppers
1 cup	coconut milk
1 tsp.	dill
1 tsp.	soya sauce
1 tsp.	worcestershire sauce
1 tsp.	gingerroot grated
1 tsp.	minced garlic

1. Clean shrimp well but leave the shells on. A messy but tasty treat is to dunk them in the sweet creamy sauce.
2. Bring all ingredients to a boil in a thick bottomed sauce pot, until shrimp are pink and curled tight.

Suggestion: Serve with lots of crusty bread for dipping and soaking up that creamy sauce. Dip shrimp into the tasty Peanut Sauce recipe (page 107) for a traditional flavouring.

Serves 4-6.

Thai food shouts of hotness and nutty flavours. Pairing barbecue nuts with ginger and garlic, is a great culinary experience. Coconut is also a familiar Thai ingredient.

Peanut Sauce

1 cup	peanut butter (smooth or crunchy)
1 tsp.	garlic minced
1 tsp.	cumin powder
1 tsp.	Chinese style fish sauce
1 tbsp.	lemon juice
1 tsp.	cayenne powder (optional)

1. Mix all well in a bowl until all is incorporated.

Peanut Sauce is a traditional condiment for many Thai recipes.

Makes approx. 1 cup.

The 1972 record for the largest tuna fish ever caught was held by Guy Blanchard and Roger Dugas of Grande-Anse on the Acadian Peninsula. This record of an 800 lb. tuna. was washed away by Camille J. Blanchard of Caraquet in 1976 when he caught a 1130 lb. tuna.

Chapter Three

How to select, clean, store and prepare shrimp

Refrigerate the shrimp as they peel easier when cool.

Cleaning: Start by pinching off the short legs along the belly of the curled part of the shrimp. Peel off the shell by placing one thumb on either side of the belly where you removed the legs and pull in an outward motion, starting at the thicker end moving down toward the tail. The tail can be left on (just the last segment) if shrimp will be served as a finger food thus acting as a handle for the person devouring them. Sometimes shrimp come with their heads still on. They are very easy to remove, grab the head with one hand and bend sideways and it will snap off where it naturally joins the body. Save the heads for stock. Some cooks prefer to cook with heads as they say they contain lots of great flavour.

After you have the shells removed, rinse quickly in cold water. Then with a sharp thin knife slice the shrimp along the backside where the shrimp bends, you will see a dark line just hiding underneath the surface. This is the digestive tract of the shrimp. With your knife gently hook the black line and remove using cold running water and/or your hands. Discard this black line matter as it may contain sand or other inedible matter. If the shrimp is tiny you may not need to do this as the black line with be too small to remove thus not affecting flavour at all.

Buying: Shrimp are sold according to their size or count. This means that the size/count is based on the average number of shrimp per pound. The smaller the number, the larger the shrimp thus resulting in fewer shrimp per pound. Large variety shrimp are size 4, which represents four shrimp to a pound. The smallest may be 160 in size or 160 shrimp per pound. There are more than 300 varieties of shrimp such as brown, pink, blue, white, tiger, & jumbo. Most fishermen will tell you that the colder the water, the smaller and more succulent the shrimp. An average size at most fish mongers would be 20 to 40 count shrimp, they are great for an all around flavour, and for ease of preparation.

Seafood

When buying shrimp, trust your nose; they should never smell fishy, nor should they smell like ammonia. An iodine aroma does not indicate spoilage, but rather the iodine-rich kelp diet of some varieties. Like most seafood, shrimp should smell of saltwater and nothing else. In terms of texture, look for firm shrimp that are moist but not slimy, with shiny, flexible-looking shells. If time and energy permit, avoid buying pre-peeled and deveined shrimp, as cleaning before freezing can diminish their flavour. Finally, avoid shrimp that have black spots on their shells which is an indication that the shrimp have begun to deteriorate, with exception of the tiger variety which may contain spots as part of their natural colouring.

Storing: Store shrimp in your fridge for up to 3 days if they are raw and 5 days once cooked.

Cooking: A variety of methods may be used. Steam for 5 to 20 minutes depending on heat source.

Bake, grill or pan fry until shrimp are curled tight and show pink in colour, approx. 5 to 10 minutes over medium to high heat.

If you are making a soup or sauce with your shrimp, you may boil the left over shells for 10 minutes in rapidly boiling water with some salt for a flavourful broth or see Simple Seafood Broth recipe on page 134.

Another technique, is to butterfly the shrimp, which means to cut them open along the backside. After you have cleaned them, score them a little deeper than you would to remove the black line you normally see there. You score deep enough to cut into the shrimp by one third of its width. This is mainly for larger shrimp where a fancy presentation is preferred. When the shrimp cooks the edges of the cut you made, curl outward thus looking similar to a butterfly with open wings, hence the name. This curling also allows for more flesh to be exposed and creates a sort of well along the center for sauces to collect.

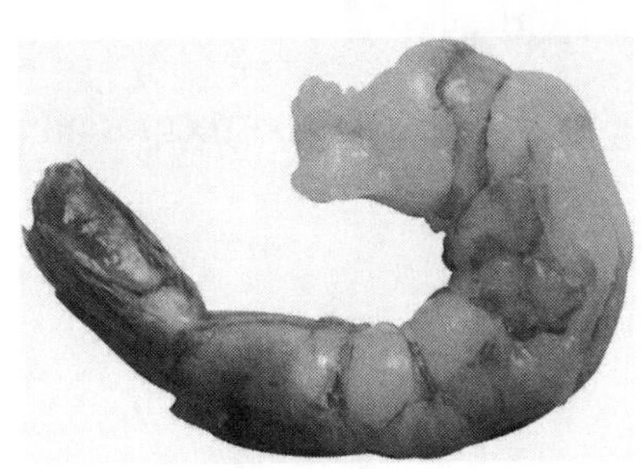

Shrimp Caesar Cocktail Salad

1/2 cup	caesar salad dressing (see page 59)
2 tbsps.	seafood cocktail sauce
1/2 tsp.	dill
1 tbsp.	soya sauce
1 tbsp.	worcestershire sauce
1/2 cup	almonds toasted
1 tbsp.	lemon juice
1	large head of romaine lettuce cut into bite size pieces
2 cups	baby spinach washed
2 lbs.	baby shrimp cleaned, cooked and cooled
1 cup	mushrooms sliced
1 cup	croutons
2 tbsps.	parmesan cheese grated
	salt & pepper to taste

1. In a bowl, mix the caesar dressing, cocktail sauce, dill, soya sauce, worcestershire sauce, almonds, lemon juice, salt and pepper. Stir until evenly mixed.
2. Place lettuce and spinach in a large salad bowl.
3. Add shrimp and mushrooms. Pour dressing mixture over all and toss.
4. Add croutons, re-toss and serve.

Suggestion: Try using one of the crouton recipes on page 58.

Serves 4-6.

Sweet and Succulent Sea Scallop Stew

1 slice	bacon
1/2 tsp.	gingerroot grated
1/2 tsp.	garlic minced
1 cup	onion minced
1/2 cup	celery minced
1/2 cup	carrots minced
2 cups	potatoes diced small
1 tbsp.	mustard
1 tbsp. ea.	soya sauce, worcestershire sauce
1 tbsp.	sesame oil
4 cups	chicken stock
1 tsp.	dill
1/4 cup	green onion minced
2 lbs.	small scallops or large ones quartered
1 cup	evaporated milk
	salt & pepper to taste

1. Cook bacon. Pat dry on paper towel and crumble. Reserve grease.
2. In the leftover bacon grease, sauté gingerroot, garlic, onion, celery, and carrots over medium heat until tender.
3. Add everything except milk and scallops into a deep pot. Make sure liquid is 3 inches over top of ingredients.
4. Cook over medium heat until potatoes are tender. Add milk and scallops and simmer for 5 more minutes.

Serves 4-8.

Maritime Mussel Stew

2 lbs.	uncooked mussels in or out of the shell
2 cups	potatoes diced
1 cup	carrots sliced round
1 cup	celery minced
1 cup	onion minced
1 cup	mushrooms thickly sliced
1 cup	turnip diced
1 tbsp.	soya sauce
1 tbsp.	worcestershire sauce
1/2 cup	fresh peas
1 cup	evaporated milk
1 cup	beef broth
2 tbsps.	clarified butter
	broth to cover
	dash of dill
	salt & pepper to taste

1. Scrub mussels well, use them in or out of shell. If discarding shells, boil them in water to make a broth. See page 134 for Seafood Broth recipe.

2. Cut all vegetables in consistent bite size pieces.

3. In a deep pot, fry everything in the butter for a few minutes (except for the mussels and milk). Fry until potatoes are tender to the fork approx. 10 minutes.

4. Add the mussels and the evaporated milk, cook for 5 more minutes until mussels open.

Suggestion: Serve with bread for dipping.

Serves 4-8.

Summer Shrimp Kabobs

24	large shrimp, butterfly cut*
8	skewer sticks or rods
24	small whole baby white onions peeled
24	pineapple wedges 1" to 2" in size
24	lime wedges (cut whole lime into 8 wedges) approximately 3 limes
24	baby mushrooms whole
24	red pepper pieces cut into 1" x 1" squares
	salt & pepper to taste

1. Have at least 3 of each item per skewer. Alternate shrimp and then a fruit and then a vegetable. Have a piece of lime next to shrimp on a skewer at all times.
2. Place on middle rack in barbecue (with cover closed) or in the oven at 425°F and cook for 15 minutes, or until shrimp are pink and curled tight.

Suggestion: serve on a bed of rice, in a pita pocket, on a soft-shell tortilla, or as a portion of a larger meal. Serve with the Summer Fruit Salsa recipe on page 85.

Serves 4-12.

Hint: Save the shrimp shells to make a lovely pink shrimp stock see page 134 for instructions.

*See page for cleaning and preparing shrimp for the butterfly method, but keep in mind it's only a suggestion for aesthetic purposes.

Drunken Side of Salmon

2 lbs.	salmon fillets
1 cup	lime juice
2	limes sliced round
1/4 cup	tequila
1 tbsp.	worcestershire sauce
1 tbsp.	soya sauce
zest	of one lemon
zest	of one lime
1 cup	chicken stock
1 tbsp.	white sugar
	salt & pepper to taste

1. Clean salmon well. Place salmon pieces evenly into a 9" x 13" casserole dish and set aside.
2. Mix soya sauce, worcestershire sauce, chicken stock, lime juice, zests, sugar and tequila into a bowl and mix well.
3. Pour mixture over fish and add salt & pepper.
4. Top with slices of lime and bake covered for 25 minutes at 400°F.

Suggestion: Serve with rice and vegetables or a side salad.

Serves 4-6.

Salmon is valued as a great source of omega-3 essential fatty acids. Check with your local physician for more about its health benefits.

Alcohol when used in recipes leaves the entire flavour of the spirit without the effects of the alcohol. The alcohol evaporates when exposed to heat, but there may be some residual alcohol so be wary of this when serving others, especially pregnant women and young children.

Barbecue Shrimp Skewers

2 lbs.	shrimp
1/2 lb.	prosciutto meat sliced as thinly as possible
	black pepper to taste

1. Clean shrimp according to instructions page 108. Place 3 shrimp per skewer.
2. Wrap a shrimp in a piece of prosciutto and weave onto the skewer.
3. Grill on high heat until shrimp are pink and curled tight and meat has become crispy.

Suggestion: Serve with some chutney or salsa.

Serves 4-8.

William Chestnut of Fredericton patented his version of the wood and canvas canoe in 1905. The Chestnut Canoe Company (1897 to 1979) was well known in Fredericton, New Brunswick.

Blueberry Cod on Citrus Rice

2 lbs.	of clean fresh cod fillets
2 cups	large blueberries cleaned
1/4 tsp.	nutmeg
1 cup	apple juice
1 cup	chicken broth
1 cup	lemon juice
1/2 cup	lime juice
1/4 cup	white sugar
1/4 cup	parsley chopped
	salt & pepper to taste

1. Place fish in a 9" x 13" casserole dish, set aside in fridge.
2. Mix all of the remaining ingredients in a saucepan and bring to a boil.
3. Remove from heat and mash berries. Strain mixture, reserving 1/2 cup for the rice recipe, pouring the rest over the fish. Bake at 400°F for 25 minutes.
4. Remove and serve with Citrus Rice recipe below.

Serves 4-6.

Citrus Rice

2 cups	rice uncooked
1/2 cup	reserved blueberry mixture(from recipe above)

1. Prepare rice according to package instructions substituting 1/2 cup of the liquid required with the reserved blueberry mixture.
2. Garnish with fresh berries, lemon and lime slices.

Suggestion: Goes well with a spicy vegetable dish.

Anchovy Garlic Butter

1 lb.	butter (room temperature)
1 tbsp.	roasted garlic mashed or 1 tsp. freshly minced
1/4 cup	anchovies minced
1 tbsp.	lemon zest

1. Cream all ingredients in a deep bowl until seasonings are incorporated.

Suggestion: Use over seafood anytime you need butter. Store in fridge for 2 weeks.

Cod is a type of fish that is enjoyed by a variety of cultures; Canadian, Newfoundland, Greek, Indian, German, Russian and French to name a few. It is available commercially in a variety of forms from dried, salt cured, fresh, and pickled, to flakes, powder, oil, and tablets. It is used in recipes from breakfast to supper to dessert. Cod is a very versatile and delicious fish.

Commercial fishing has long been the sturdy backbone for many New Brunswick communities. Many people are employed in this industry which spans from the Gulf of Saint Lawrence to the Bay of Fundy. The main catch for most fishermen is the great Atlantic lobster. Crab and herring are close in the running for second place. Salmon is the largest domestic farming resource we have for the fishing industry. Mussels and oysters from the Gulf of Saint Lawrence claim their fame in the cold waters there.

Brunswick Snow Crab Legs with Strawberries

16	large crab legs
1 cup	whole strawberries
2 cups	cold water
1 tbsp.	soya sauce
1 tbsp.	worcestershire sauce
1	lemon sliced round
1/4 cup	white sugar

1. Scrub legs.
2. Place all ingredients except for crab in a deep pot and stir well until sugar is dissolved.
3. Place crab legs on top of mixture making sure open end of legs are on top facing up.
4. Cover the pot and bring to a boil.
5. Reduce heat to low and simmer 10 minutes covered.
6. Remove from heat and remove legs.

Suggestion: Serve with melted butter. Reserve berry mixture and use for dipping.

Serves 4-6.

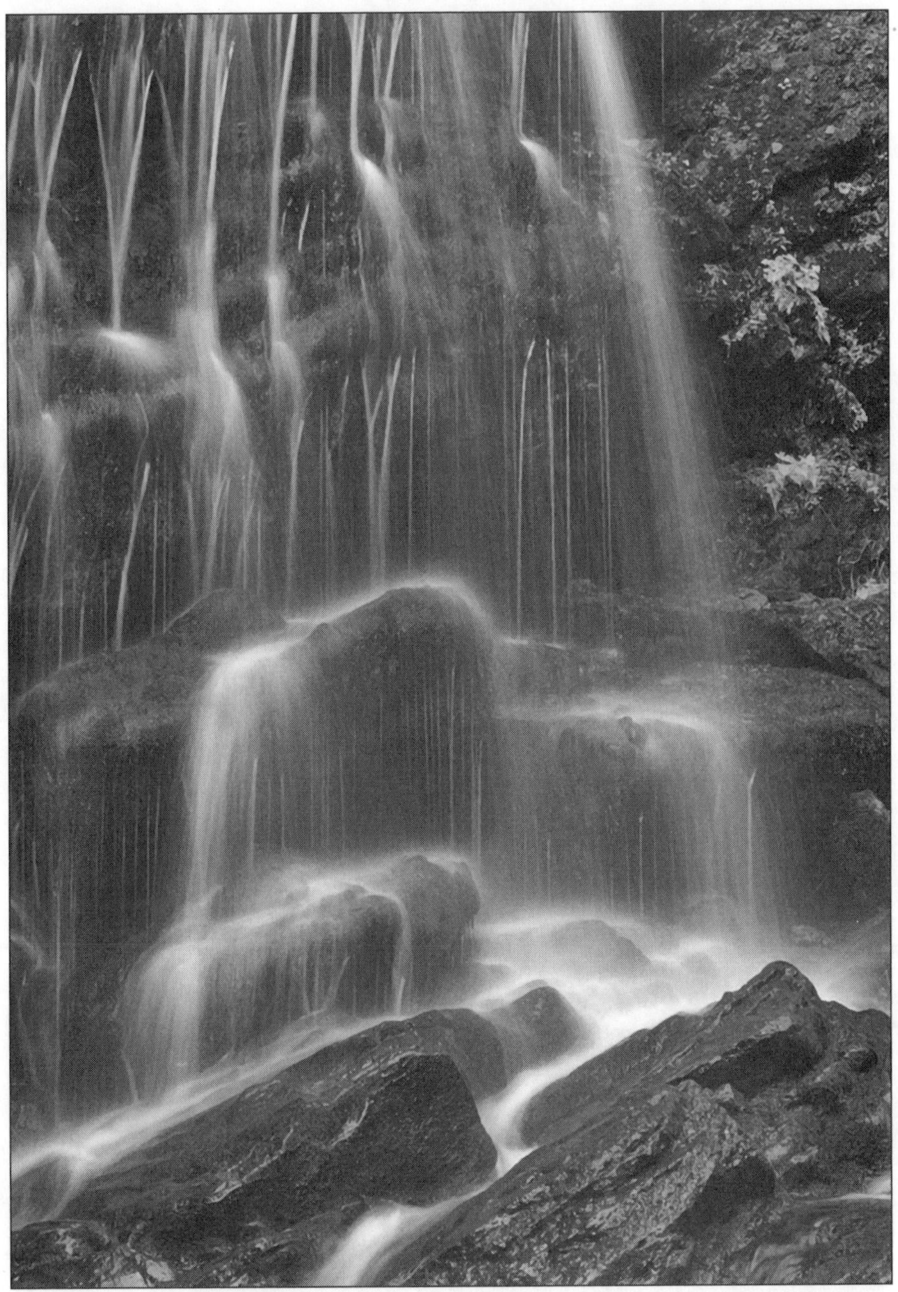

The Fundy Trail has great foliage and fall is a perfect time to view the rolling red and gold landscapes. This scenic season has the province covered in a canopy of autumn kissed country roads and can be best experienced in a horse drawn carriage ride down a quiet country lane. Photo: Paul Evans, Evans Communications Inc.

Raspberry Oysters Rockefeller

4 lbs.	oysters raw
1 cup	fresh raspberries*
1/2 cup	apple juice
1 tbsp.	soya sauce
1 tbsp.	worcestershire sauce
1 tbsp.	butter
1/4 cup	lemon juice
1/2 tsp.	dill
1 tbsp.	lemon zest finely minced
1/4 cup	fennel or anise bulb finely grated
1/2 cup ea.	onion, celery (finely minced)
1 tsp.	licorice flavoured liquor (such as Pernod, Anisette, or Ouzo)
	salt & pepper to taste

1. Clean oysters well. Open, making sure to retain their juices.
2. Place oysters on the half shell and lay as flat as possible in a shallow 9" x 13" baking dish. Set aside.
3. In a medium mixing bowl, place the raspberries, apple juice, soya sauce, fennel/anise bulb, worcestershire sauce, dill, lemon juice and zest. Stir well until even and set aside.
4. Sauté the onion and celery in the butter until they are soft and tender with juices bubbling.
5. Add the fruit mixture, toss well. Bring mixture to a rolling boil for 3 minutes. Remove from heat, add liquor, and restir.

...continued on next page

6. Spoon 1 tbsp. of fruit mixture over top of each oyster. Any leftover can be reserved for a dipping sauce.

7. Broil in oven at 450°F for 20 minutes or until topping starts to roast.

*Try using your favourite variety of summer fruit for this dish; strawberries, blueberries, apple or blackberries.

Suggestion: Serve with a nice side salad or over a bed of rice. Toss in some crusty bread to soak up all those juices.

Serves 4-8.

Oyster beds are found along river mouths and inlets on the southern Gulf of St. Lawrence and the Northumberland Straight all the way to Cape Breton. The two halves of the shell are equal in size but the top one is flat while the bottom one is curved to house the oyster. Their outside shell is rough and sculptured in appearance. The colour varies from brown, grey, green to white. The inside of the shell is superbly smooth with a dull white finish. Spring and fall are the two seasons for harvest and they range in size from 3 to 10 inches in diameter.

An oyster can take up to 7 years to reach market size. They have slightly salty but plump flesh. The shape and size determines the quality or grade. They are harvested with hand held rakes. Oysters require air to breathe and are kept around 5°C / 40°F. Oyster juice is a prized item and you can find it bottled in any grocery store. When shucking oysters reserve as much juice as you can for your dish. During oyster season you may find oyster shucking contests at local festivals.

Lobster Cream Bisque with Fiddleheads

1 cup	mushrooms thinly sliced
2 cups	potatoes diced small
1 cup	fiddleheads well cleaned and diced
1/2 tsp.	lemon zest
2 cups	cream (whipping cream, evaporated milk, cereal cream or buttermilk)
1 lb.	lobster meat diced
1 lb.	lobster knuckles & claws in the shell cleaned well (raw)
1 tbsp.	garlic minced
1 cup	onion finely minced
1/2 cup	celery finely minced
1 tbsp.	soya sauce
1 tbsp.	worcestershire sauce
1/2 tsp.	dill
1/2 tsp.	nutmeg
1 tbsp.	bacon bits fried crispy with grease reserved
2 tbsps.	clarified butter see recipe page 69
	water to cover
	salt & pepper to taste

1. If using lobster in the shell, reserve shells to produce great stock. See Simple Seafood Broth recipe page 134.
2. Place the bacon grease and butter in a frying pan. Over medium high heat, fry the onions, mushrooms, celery and garlic until golden brown.

...continued on next page

3. Add potatoes, and fry for 2 minutes. Remove from heat and place all into a deep stock pot. Cover mixture with water or stock until water is 2 inches above ingredients.

4. Add herbs, and seasonings. Boil over high heat until potatoes are half cooked, add fiddleheads and lobster. Reduce heat to medium and cook until fiddleheads are tender, about 10 minutes.

5. Add milk, stir well and let sit 5 minutes on lowest heat checking every few minutes to ensure milk does not burn.

Suggestion: To serve with dumplings stewed in the pot, add dumplings before you add the milk and continue cooking until dumplings are 3/4 cooked. Add milk and increase heat to medium, cover pot and cook until dumplings are ready, about 5 more minutes. Serve puff pastry cut with seafood shaped cookie cutters as a replacement for breadsticks or biscuits. Or cut biscuits or toasted garlic bread into seafood shapes.

Serves 4-8.

Almost 50% of the world's lobster supply is harvested from the Atlantic waters. The fishery is based on rotating regions to allow for natural replenishment of the stocks. Lobstermen in NB pride themselves in maintaining a sustainable industry. It takes a lobster 4 to 7 years to reach the size for market. Lobsters molt as they grow wiggling out of their hard shell so they can grow a new and bigger shell. This wiggling or molting takes on average 5 to 20 minutes, then the lobster drinks large amounts of water for the next few hours to gain weight helping it grow bigger. After purchasing, lobsters are best stored between 33 to 40°C or 91 to 104°F. They live in salt water and breathe air. They must be alive when you cook them. Some folk say the cold deep waters of the North Atlantic add a taste you can't describe or replace.

Garlic Shrimp over Pasta

450g	angel hair pasta
2 lbs.	small shrimp uncooked
1 cup	zucchini julienned with peel on
1/2 cup	garlic sliced thinly
1/4 cup	crushed pineapple
1/2 cup	plum tomatoes chopped
1 tbsp.	soya sauce
1 tbsp.	worcestershire sauce
1 tbsp.	lemon juice
1 tbsp.	clarified butter recipe (page 69) or olive oil
	salt & pepper to taste

1. Cook pasta according to package directions.
2. Clean and prepare shrimp according to instructions page 108.
3. In a deep frying pan, sauté garlic for 1 minute over medium-high heat.
4. Add zucchini and fry for 1 more minute stirring constantly.
5. Add tomatoes, pineapple, soya sauce, worcestershire sauce and lemon juice. Simmer for 5 minutes stirring twice.
6. Add shrimp and cook for 5 minutes. Serve over a bed of angel hair pasta.

Serves 4-8.

In 1900 a man named Joseph Clark from the St.George region registered his invention for the key opening can, which is used today on many seafood, and luncheon meats. In 1932, Henry Austin from Blacks Harbour invented the sardine can. It was perfect for carrying in your lunch box, easy to open with the key and very lightweight. Connors Brothers Limited is the largest sardine plant in Canada. It played a big part in the development of the key opening can, which is world famous today.

Salmon Breakfast Omelette

4	large eggs
1/4 cup	red onion finely minced
1 tsp.	garlic minced
1/2 lb.	salmon pieces cooked and cooled
pinch	of dill flakes
1 tbsp.	butter
1/4 cup	cheese of choice, grated (optional)
	salt & pepper to taste

1. Separate four egg whites into a separate bowl. Beat until stiff peaks form. Set aside in fridge.

2. In another bowl, beat remaining egg yolks until frothy. Add garlic, dill and salt and pepper.

3. Fold in egg whites.

4. Melt butter in frying pan over medium to high heat. Sauté the onion until tender and slightly transparent, add garlic and fry for 1 more minute.

4. Pour in egg mixture, quickly sprinkle with salmon pieces.

5. Gently stir as egg cooks, pulling in the sides towards the center of the pan for 2 minutes.

6. Cover immediately and let continue cooking for 2 minutes. Turn off heat and let sit for 2 minutes off heat source.

Serves 2-3.

Campbellton is famous for its salmon from the Restigouche River. They celebrate each year with local cultural festivities. Try some salmon; cold smoked, maple cured or just thrown on the barbecue. This region is also well known for its exceptional winter skiing adventures as well.

Chapter Three

Creamy Seafood Casserole Bake

This dish can be made with any single type of seafood like crab, cod, salmon, scallop, shrimp, sole, etc.… or a combination of any. The recipe is basic and then I have listed the variations for each specific type of seafood such as a cheese or vegetable that will enhance its flavour. If you use a shellfish variety check out page 134 about making fabulous flavoured fish stock from the emptied shells.

1 recipe	thin béchamel sauce (page 91)
3 lbs.	seafood of choice, uncooked see specific seafood type for cheese amount listed at the end of the recipe*
1/2 cup	onion finely minced
1/2 cup	celery finely minced
1 tbsp.	garlic minced
1/4 cup	lemon juice
1/2 cup	18 % cream
1 tsp.	dill flakes
1 tsp.	soya sauce
1 tbsp.	worcestershire sauce
1 tbsp.	clarified butter recipe (page 69)
2 lbs.	mashed potatoes cooled
	salt & pepper to taste

1. Clean seafood and pat dry, set aside in fridge until ready to cook. Prepare mashed potatoes using the cream and whip them well. Set aside. Have cold béchamel sauce ready to use.

…continued on next page

2. In a hot frying pan, add the butter and sauté the seafood for 2 minutes per side gaining some caramelization and flavour. This is not to cook the seafood just to add some colour and flavour enhancement. Remove seafood pieces and spread them evenly in a 9" x 13" casserole dish.
3. Fry the onion, celery, and garlic until slightly golden. Remove from heat and add the lemon juice, dill, salt, pepper, soya sauce, and worcestershire sauce. Pour this mixture evenly over the seafood.
4. Sprinkle cheese over seafood evenly. Spread a thin layer of mashed potatoes over top of the seafood leaving an open border of 1" from the outside edge of the dish.
5. Pour béchamel sauce over top ensuring it runs down into the casserole dish through the one inch border you left open around the edge. Bake at 350°F until sauce bubbles in middle of pan or top becomes golden brown. About 20 to 45 minutes.

You may need to add a little water or stock to the casserole base before adding the potatoes on top; thin to desired consistency. The dish will thicken during cooking and again as it cools.

Serves 6-10.

***Seafood varieties:** Use one or a combination of the following:

Cod Fish, Sole, Haddock – Cut fish into 2" cubes, 1 cup of old cheddar cheese grated.

Shrimp – clean, devein, and butterfly them making sure to remove all shells. 1/2 cup parmesan cheese grated.

Scallop – use baby ones or cut up the larger variety, 1/2 cup parmesan cheese grated and 1/4 cup cheddar.

Crab – remove meat from shell, 1/4 cup parmesan cheese grated.

Clams, mussels, oysters – remove meat from shell reserving any liquid for your dish, 1/4 cup parmesan cheese grated, 1 tsp. licorice flavoured liquor or extract.

Linguine Alfredo with Mussels

1 lb.	mussels per person, raw in shell
450g	cooked linguine noodles, spinach variety
1 tsp.	garlic butter
1/2 cup	whipping cream
1/2 cup	whole milk
1 tbsp.	soya sauce
1 tbsp.	worcestershire sauce
1/2 cup	parmesan cheese shredded
1 cup	baby spinach julienned
1/2 tsp.	lemon zest
dash	of dill
	salt & pepper to taste

1. Clean and prepare mussels, see page 138.
2. Place all ingredients, except for the cheese into a thick-bottomed saucepan and bring to a boil over medium high heat. Add the cheese and stir well until slightly thickened.
3. Remove from heat and serve over julienned spinach.

Suggestion: Serve with toasted garlic bread.

Serves 4-6.

Sweet Summer Scallop Skewers

24	large scallops
8	skewer sticks
16	pineapple wedges 1 to 2 inches in size
2	lemons whole cut into 8 wedges each
1 tsp.	dill dried
2 tbsps.	brown sugar
1 tbsp.	soya sauce
1 tbsp.	worcestershire sauce
	salt & pepper to taste

1. Clean scallops and set aside.
2. Mix 1 tbsp. sugar, soya sauce, worcestershire sauce and dill in a bowl until combined.
3. Dip scallops into this sauce mixture until all are coated.
4. Thread skewers as follows: lemon, scallop, pineapple, scallop, lemon, scallop, pineapple.
5. Make sure to use 3 scallops per skewer.
6. Sprinkle the skewers with the remaining sugar.
7. Preheat grill. Grill or bake at 450°F until scallops are golden approx. 10 to 25 minutes.

Serves 4-8.

Barbecue Lime and Tequila Salmon

4	salmon fillets or steaks
1/2 cup	lime juice
1 tbsp.	lime zest
1/4 cup	tequila
1 tsp.	black pepper
1 tbsp.	soya sauce
1 tbsp.	worcestershire sauce
1/2 cup	dark brown sugar
1 tbsp.	fresh coriander/cilantro minced
	salt to taste

1. Heat grill to medium.
2. Clean fish and place on a cookie sheet, skin side down. Cover and place in fridge.
3. In a bowl, mix the lime juice and zest, tequila, pepper, soya sauce, coriander, worcestershire sauce, brown sugar and salt. Stir until the sugar is dissolved.
4. Brush the salmon pieces with this mixture, making sure to coat them generously.
5. Let sit for 5 minutes.
6. Grill on top rack in barbecue, skin side down, until cooked.
7. If there is any sauce left over use it to baste during the cooking process.

Suggestion: Serve with a potato salad or rice.

Serves 4

Seafood

There is another shellfish out there some of you may have had the experience of tasting, the bay quahaug. It lives in warm and shallow bay areas from the Miramichi to Nova Scotia. This shellfish has a thick, heavy slightly inflated shell with numerous concentric growth lines. Its colour is dull white and ranges in size from 3 to 11 inches in diameter. Small quahaugs are usually sold fresh and the larger ones are usually shucked, canned and sold for their meat.

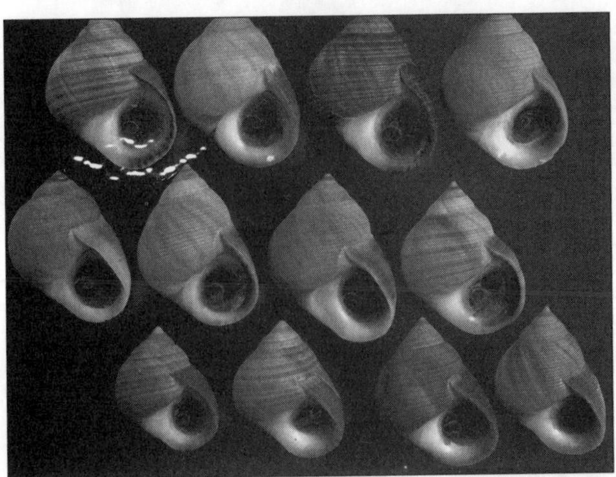

The common periwinkle, or snail as it is better known, can be found at tide level along NB's rocky seaweed covered shores, and on sand and mud flats everywhere. They are usually no more than 1 to 3 inches in diameter with an olive to brownish and sometimes grey black shell. They can close their shells by retracting the large bottom foot. They are usually picked by party goers during a summer picnic and boiled in salted water for a few minutes and then popped out with the twist of a pin. Dredged in drawn butter they make a delicious snack.

Fisherman Codfish Cakes

This recipe is the basic method for making fish cakes *but I have also offered you the method to make an assortment of cakes using many varieties or combinations of seafood. The variations are based on what ingredients enhance each type of seafood or shellfish. Add the extra items to the potato mixture. You make a seafood mixture, form it into patties, and then cook until crispy.*

4 cups	codfish cooked and flaked apart
1/4 cup	mayonnaise
1 tbsp.	soya sauce
1/2 tsp.	dill
1 tsp.	lemon juice
1/4 cup	onion puréed
1 cup	fine dry bread crumbs
1 egg	beaten
1 tbsp.	worcestershire sauce
2 cups	mashed potatoes cooled
1/4 cup	clarified butter recipe (page 69)
2 cups	cornflake crumbs finely crushed
	salt & pepper to taste

1. Clean codfish of any bones and such. Flake apart into small pieces. Most of the fish can be diced small; some of the different varieties like salmon, and crab are better flaked apart. Set aside in fridge until ready to use.

2. Place potatoes in a deep bowl, mix in the mayonnaise, soya sauce, dill, lemon juice, onion, bread crumbs, egg, worcestershire sauce, salt and pepper. Fold in the seafood and mix until evenly distributed.

...continued on next page

*For each specific type of seafood add the extra ingredients listed below during step 2.

3. Use a 1/4 cup; 1/2 cup measuring cup; or ice cream scoop to portion out patties. Form patties with your hands. Use cold water, or lightly grease your hands if the mixture becomes too sticky, or return mixture to the fridge for 30 minutes to stiffen up.

4. Place salmon cakes on a cookie sheet, and brush cakes with clarified butter. Roll salmon cakes in cornflake crumbs and return to the cookie sheet. Bake at 350°F for 30 minutes or until golden and crispy.

Suggestion: They may be served as a side dish, main menu item or made very small and used as hors d'oeuvres.

Makes 8 to 36 cakes.

***Seafood Variations:**

Hungryman Halibut Fishburger - you could use haddock; or sole as well; – add 1 tsp. lemon juice; 1/4 cup cheddar cheese grated.

Crusty Crab Cakes – add 2 tbsps. lemon juice; 1/4 cup Swiss cheese grated; 1/2 tsp. nutmeg grated.

Zingy Salmon Circles – add 2 tbsps. lemon juice; 1 tsp. dill flakes; 1/2 tsp. gingerroot grated.

Succulent Scallop Snowballs – add 1/2 cup coconut finely shredded; 2 tbsps. lime juice; 1 tsp. lime zest.

Luscious Lobster Medallions – 1 clove garlic minced; 1 tsp. capers minced; 1 tbsp. lemon juice; 4 slices of bacon cooked, drained & crumbled.

The Bay of Fundy is the best visual experience you can walk through. The glacial carved rocks are formed from 100 billion tons of water which rise and fall as part of nature's power and grace of gravity. These rock formations are beautiful to look at.

Simple Seafood Broth

This is a way to get the most flavour out of any seafood dish you have or make. When you use seafood for a specific recipe, save the shells or bones and make some very flavourful broth. This can be made with any type of shellfish, mussels, clams, lobster, shrimp, etc... and for fish, the bones and skin carry the flavour.

2 lbs. or more	seafood shells or bones of seafood/shellfish raw or cooked (all meat removed)
2 tbsps.	peppercorns
1	lemon cut in half
3	stalks of celery
2	whole carrots unpeeled
1	medium sized onion unpeeled
2	medium sized potatoes unpeeled
1	piece of seaweed if you have it (3" x 6" piece)
1	beach rock from under the ocean water freshly picked and scrubbed with soap first (optional).
	water to cover approx. 4 to 12 liters

1. Take shells and roast them in the oven, or on the barbecue, until the shell, skin or bones start to blacken. Roast at 450°F to 550°F for 10 to 35 minutes. Remove from oven.

2. Add all ingredients listed above into a deep stockpot and cover with water. Bring to a boil and reduce to simmer for 1 hour.

3. Strain well and use for soups, chowders, casseroles, sauces and dips.

Mom's Mussel and Barley Stew

3 lbs.	mussels raw in shell
1 cup	small shell shaped pasta uncooked
2 cups	chopped stewed tomatoes
1/2 cup	barley uncooked
1/4 cup	crispy fried bacon minced
1 cup	onion finely minced
1/2 cup	leek sliced round
1 cup	zucchini diced small
1 cup	mushrooms thinly sliced
1/2 cup	carrots finely minced
1 cup	white wine
2 cups	chicken broth
1 tbsp.	dried basil flakes
1/2 tsp.	oregano
1/2 tsp.	cumin
1 tsp.	dill
dash	of olive oil
	salt & pepper to taste

1. Clean and prepare mussels according to technique on page 138.

2. Place everything into a large stock pot.

3. Bring to a boil, reduce heat to low and simmer until barley is tender to the bite.

Suggestion: Serve with bread for dipping or dumplings.

Serves 4-8.

Co Co St. Jacques Scallop Bisque

2 lbs.	uncooked scallops (shells removed)
1/4 cup	clarified butter recipe (page 69)
6	slices bacon
1 cup	onion minced
1 tsp.	dill flakes
1/2 tsp.	nutmeg grated
1 tbsp.	garlic minced
1 tsp.	gingerroot shredded
1 cup	18 % cream
2 cups	potatoes diced
1/2 cup	celery minced
1 tbsp.	lemon juice
1 cup	evaporated milk
	water, fish or chicken stock to cover
	salt & pepper to taste

1. Clean scallops well. Set aside.
2. Fry bacon and reserve grease.
3. Add bacon grease and butter to the frying pan over medium to high heat.
4. Fry scallops until golden brown, then remove from heat. Pat dry of fat.
5. Place one and a half pounds of scallops into a bowl and set aside. Reserve 1 tbsp. of bacon grease. Place the other 1/2 pound of scallops into a bowl and set aside.

...continued on next page

6. Fry onion, garlic and gingerroot in the same frying pan with the reserved bacon grease for 2 minutes over high heat. Remove from heat, drain off any remaining bacon grease. Discard any remaining grease once cooled.

7. In the stockpot, combine all ingredients except scallops.

8. Simmer over low to medium heat until potatoes fall apart.

9. Add scallops and cook for 5 minutes.

10. Purée soup with hand blender for 5 minutes. If you do not have a hand blender you can use a food processor or regular blender but be careful when working with hot liquids, make sure the hot liquid is vented. You can always cool the soup, purée and then reheat.

11. Reheat the reserved half pound of scallops just until they are warm. Chop roughly and sprinkle over top of each bowl just before serving.

Serves 4-8.

Note: Reduce the fat content by using a nonstick pan, and discarding the bacon fat in step 3. The cream and milk may also be substituted for a lower fat version.

New Brunswick has over 300 bird species on its sea washed sh Rare birds like the bald eagle and, the endangered piping p find sanctuary in New Brunswick. While bird watching, sear beaches and shores for fossils.

Mussels - How to select, clean, store and prepare

Serving size in the shell

1/2 to 1 lb. as a hors-d'oeuvre
1 lb. as a side dish
2 to 3 lbs. as a main meal

Buying: Select clean looking mussels with the shell on. When displayed on ice the shells should be closed. Purchase as fresh as possible from a reputable fish monger. The shells if still on should be almost completely closed to indicate live and active mussels. Make sure your fish monger puts air in the bag for the trip home as mussels need air to stay alive. Mussels usually sit partially open when out of water. When a mussel is open gently tap it on the counter top to see if it closes its shell. If the shell does not close, the mussel is dead, and is not suitable for eating; it must be discarded. Local mussels have seasons that are best and safest for harvesting, check with your local department of fisheries for the best times to go mussel digging.

Storing: store mussels in the fridge in a shallow pan or bowl covered with a wet cloth. DO NOT ADD TAP WATER to the mussels as this will kill them. Mussels will keep in your fridge for 2 to 3 days.

Cleaning: mussels may come fairly clean especially the cultivated ones, but often there is still some sand in the shells and wooly looking hairs called "beards" still attached. Scrub shells lightly with a brush to remove any dirt. Pull off all beards. Quickly rinse shells under tap water being careful not to soak them or this will kill them.

If you prefer to remove mussels from shells before cooking, you will have to force open the shell with a shucking knife available at your fish market. The juice inside the shell is very flavourful so try to shuck cleaned mussels over a bowl to preserve juice. Mussels in the shell add a decorative look to seafood dishes.

Cooking: A variety of methods may be used.
Steam for 5 to 20 minutes depending on heat source.
Bake in oven or on barbecue until they pop open, approx. 10 minutes on 425°F.
After cooking all mussels should open up, discard any mussels that do not open up during the cooking process, they are not safe to eat.
If you are making a soup or sauce with your mussels, you may boil the left over shells for 10 minutes in rapid boiling water with salt for flavourful broth or see Simple Seafood Broth recipe on page 134.

Succulent Seafood Lasagna

Sauce mixture:

4 cups	of meatless spaghetti sauce
1 cup	mushrooms sliced
1/2 cup	onion minced
1 cup	seafood cocktail sauce
1 tbsp.	worcestershire sauce
1 tbsp.	soya sauce
1 tbsp.	dried basil
3 cups	seafood (such as cod, haddock, shrimp, scallops, clams, mussels, salmon, etc.)
dash	of nutmeg
dash	of dried dill
1 cup	stock (fish, beef, chicken or vegetable)
1 tbsp.	olive oil

16 strips	of cooked and cooled lasagna noodles
2 cups	cottage cheese
2 cups	mozzarella cheese shredded
	salt & pepper to taste

1. Sauté the mushrooms and onion in the olive oil until golden.
2. In a large stock pot, bring all of the remaining sauce ingredients to a slow simmer. Let sauce simmer on lowest heat until it reduces by one third.
3. Mix cottage and mozzarella cheese together in a bowl and set aside.
4. In a 9" x 13" lasagna dish, spread a thin layer of sauce over the bottom.

...continued on next page

5. Layer across the pan 4 strips of noodles, and then layer on half of the cheese over top of the noodles, then repeat with sauce again.

6. Repeat step 5 until all ingredients are used.

7. Bake 30 to 45 minutes at 350°F until sauce bubbles.

Serves 4-8.

Did you know that lobsters prefer deep dark places and are most active at night which makes them hard for scientists to study. Did you know a lobster has two bladders and that they are found in the head of the lobster.

From the Bay of Chaleur to the Bay of Fundy, the waters of New Brunswick offer locals and visitors alike some of the finest and freshest seafood around. There is an abundance of succulent seafood throughout the coastal communities so make sure to partake in this incredible coastal culinary experience. Visit Campbellton during late June and early July for their annual Salmon Festival spanning a few weeks. This festival originated in Canada's centennial year, 1967. The months of June, July and August are filled with festivals celebrating the cultures that established our province.

Lemon Dill Butter

1 lb.	butter (room temperature)
zest	of whole lemon
1 tbsp.	dill
	black pepper to taste

1. In a deep medium sized bowl, add all ingredients and cream until seasonings are evenly incorporated in the butter.

Suggestion: Use anywhere you would use butter. Will keep in fridge for 2 weeks.

Makes approx. 2 cups.

Clams usually are found near the mouth of rivers and inlets and near some beaches. They live in the sand and mud around midtide level. They come usually in an oval shaped shell which is thin and brittle and chalky white in colour. They cannot close their shells entirely due to the long neck that extends beyond the edge of their shells.

Maple Mussel Cream Pie

1 double	Savoury Pie Crust recipe (page 194)
1 cup	mushrooms sliced
1 cup	sweet onion minced
1/2 cup	maple syrup
1/4 cup	whipping cream
1/2 cup	mozzarella cheese shredded
2 cups	whipped* potatoes cold
1 tsp.	cornstarch
2 tbsps.	clarified butter recipe (page 69)
2 lbs.	mussels shelled with juice
dash	of dill and nutmeg
	salt & pepper to taste

1. Clean and prepare mussels as per instructions on page 138. Scrape out mussel with knife or spoon making sure to reserve any natural juices.

2. Layer pie plate with one of the pie crusts. Set aside.

3. Sauté the onion and mushrooms in the butter until slightly cooked. Set aside to cool.

3. In a deep bowl, mix mussels with sautéed vegetables, add maple syrup, whipping cream, salt, pepper, dill and nutmeg. Stir well.

4. Pour mixture into the pie shell. Sprinkle cornstarch over all and cover with mozzarella, followed by potatoes.

5. Cover tightly with top crust leaving a vent hole. Bake at 425°F for 15 to 25 minutes until juice bubbles from pie.

Makes one 9 inch pie.

* Whipped potatoes are regular mashed potatoes with extra whipping cream and or butter. They are beaten by a hand mixer so they are very aerated, fluffy and creamy.

Blueberry Mustard Shrimp

1 cup	blueberries, freshly mashed, jam, or jelly
1/2 cup	mustard
1 tsp.	fresh dill
1 tbsp.	lemon juice
1 tsp.	lemon zest
32	jumbo tiger shrimp
2 cups	shrimp stock
2 cups	onion sliced round
1 tbsp. ea.	soya sauce, worcestershire sauce
	salt & pepper to taste

1. Clean shrimp, peel, and devein them. Reserve shrimp shells for making stock. Set shrimp aside.
2. Boil shrimp shells with enough water for 15 minutes to produce 2 cups of stock. Discard shells. Strain stock. Set aside.
3. Line bottom of shallow baking dish with onion.
4. Place shrimp over top of onion.
5. In a mixing bowl, place the blueberries, mustard, dill, lemon juice, zest, stock, worcestershire sauce and soya sauce. Add salt & pepper to taste. Mix well and pour over shrimp making sure every shrimp gets coated in this mixture.
6. Cover with foil and bake for 30 minutes on 450°F.
7. Remove shrimp and serve with rice and a fruit salsa. The remaining onion and fruit mixture can be served as a garnish or relish to accompany the dish.

Serves 4-8.

Lobster Clubhouse

1 lb.	lobster meat (claws, knuckles, or tails)
1/4 cup	tartar sauce
4 slices	bacon
8 slices	tomato
2 leaves	lettuce
1/4 cup	cheddar cheese grated
1 tsp.	lemon juice
4	slices of bread
	salt & pepper to taste

1. Chop lobster into bite size morsels. Place in a bowl. Sprinkle with the lemon juice and pepper. Stir well until lemon juice is soaked up by the lobster meat.

2. Fry bacon until crispy, discard grease and pat dry.

3. Layer sandwich in the following order: Use half of the ingredients since you are making two sandwiches. Spread one slice of bread with some tartar sauce. Add the cheese, bacon, lettuce, tomato and lobster. Spread the second slice of bread with tartar sauce and place on top of the sandwich fillings. Repeat.

Serves 2.

Wild blueberries have been harvested for many generations here in New Brunswick. Approx. 10 million pounds are produced yearly by local farmers. August is the month of harvest and fields cover the hillsides everywhere. Blueberries are sold, fresh, frozen and in any cooked form that you can imagine.

Hot 'n Spicy Shrimp Rub

2 tbsps.	cumin powder
2 tbsps.	curry powder
2 tbsps.	black pepper
1 tsp.	salt
2 tbsps.	coriander powder
2 tsps.	cayenne pepper
1 tbsp.	garlic powder
1 tsp.	basil powder
1 tsp.	crushed chilies

1. Clean and prepare shrimp according to instructions on page 108.
2. Stir all in a deep bowl until even mixed. Sprinkle over shrimp and rub so all shrimp are coated well.
3. Cook on a barbecue or broil in the oven until shrimp are pink and curled tight.

Suggestion: Try on any type of seafood or meat.

Makes approx. 3/4 cup of rub mix, suitable for 2 to 3 lbs. of shrimp.

Commercial fishing is the fourth largest industry in New Brunswick after forestry, mining, and agriculture. Lobster, crab and salmon are the largest crops in fishing.

Blue mussels live along coastlines and river mouths. They attach themselves with their thread like beards to rocks, wharf pilings or other salt water submerged surfaces. Mussels are harvested mainly through March, April, May and then again in October and November.

Scrumptious Shellfish Soup

2 liters	chicken stock
1/2 cup	carrots
1 cup	red pepper minced
1 cup	chopped plum tomatoes
1 tsp.	basil
1 tsp.	dill
1/2 cup	green onion
1/2 cup	lemon juice
zest	of 1 lemon
1 tbsp.	parsley
1 tbsp.	garlic minced
1/2 cup	red onion minced
2 cups	shrimp
1 cup	lobster meat
1 cup	baby scallops
2 cups	mussels out of shell
1 cup	crab meat
1 tbsp.	sesame seeds
	salt & pepper to taste

1. Place everything except the seafood in a deep stock pot and bring to a boil until the onions are transparent.
2. Add all seafood and cook for 20 minutes over medium heat. Add sesame seeds and serve.
3. You may need to add additional stock as the vegetables cook and the liquid evaporates. Keep the liquid over the seafood by at least 1 inch at all times.

Serves 6-10.

Lobster and Spinach Stuffed Mushrooms

1 lb.	lobster meat
1 lb.	baby spinach
1 cup	cream cheese
1 tsp.	dill
1 tsp.	lemon zest
	mushrooms*
1 tsp.	garlic minced
	salt & pepper to taste

1. Clean and wash spinach and set aside.
2. Clean and prepare mushrooms by removing their stems so you may stuff them full of the cheese mixture.
3. Place all ingredients except the lobster into a food processor or blender and purée until smooth.
4. Add lobster and pulse or blend slowly so lobster remains a little chunky.
5. Stuff mushrooms and place on a lined cookie sheet or a 9" x 13" casserole dish.
6. Bake at 450°F or broil until cheese is golden brown in color. Try cooking on the barbecue for a smoky flavour for those summer parties. This should take approx. 10 to 35 minutes.

***Mushrooms:** Use 12 large stuffing mushrooms which can be found at most local grocery stores. If using button baby mushrooms you will need at least 2 lbs. If using the Portobello variety use 6.

Hint: The stems from the mushrooms may be incorporated back into the food processor with the cheese mixture or saved for another meal or stock pot.

Serves 4-10.

Creamy Mussel Chowder

2 cups	potatoes diced
1 tbsp.	soya sauce
1 tbsp.	worcestershire sauce
1/2 cup	onion diced
1/2 cup	celery diced
1/2 cup	carrots diced
1/2 cup	mushrooms sliced
2 cups	chicken stock
1 tsp.	dill
1/2 tsp.	oregano
1/4 tsp.	nutmeg
1 cup	18% cream
3 lbs.	uncooked mussels out of the shell with juice reserved
1 lb.	uncooked mussels in shell
	salt and pepper to taste

1. Clean and prepare mussels as per instructions page 138.
2. Place potatoes, soya sauce, worcestershire sauce, onion, celery, carrots, mushrooms, chicken stock, dill, oregano, and nutmeg into a deep pot.
3. Cover with cold water until liquid is 3 inches above the ingredients.
4. Simmer over low heat until potatoes are tender.
5. Add cream and all of the mussels.
6. Continue to cook until mussels in the shell open up, about 10 minutes.

Serves 4-8.

Thai Crusted Fish Fillet

4	fish* fillets
1 cup	hot barbecue peanuts
1 tbsp.	worcestershire sauce
1 tbsp.	soya sauce
2 tbsps.	garlic minced
1 tsp.	gingerroot grated
1 tbsp.	lemon juice
1 tsp.	sesame seeds raw
1 tbsp.	cornstarch
	salt & pepper to taste

1. Crush barbecue peanuts in food processor with 1 tbsp. cornstarch. If grinding nuts by hand omit the cornstarch altogether. Set aside.
2. In a bowl, mix the worcestershire sauce, soya sauce, garlic, gingerroot, lemon juice, sesame seeds, salt and pepper. Stir until evenly mixed.
3. Spread fish fillets on a shallow baking dish and brush the wet mixture over the top of each fillet with a pastry brush.
4. Cover each fillet with a layer of crushed peanuts. Pack down to form a crust on top.
5. Bake at 450°F uncovered for 20 minutes until crust is golden and fish is cooked. Let fish rest for 3 minutes after removing from oven.

Suggestion: Serve with a citrus and or creamy milk based rice dish like Creamy Coconut Rice, see recipe page 55.

Serves 4.

*Use fish of choice (salmon, Boston blue, cod, haddock, trout, tuna, etc...)

Greek Shrimp with Lemon Mint Cream Sauce

2 lbs.	uncooked shrimp, shells removed
1/2 cup	sour cream
1 tsp.	hot pepper flakes
1/4 cup	icing sugar sifted well
2 tbsps.	lemon juice
1 tsp.	lemon zest finely shredded
1 tbsp.	mint leaves minced
1 tsp.	jalapeno pepper diced small
1/4 cup	onion finely minced
1/4 cup	celery minced
1/4 cup	garlic minced
1 tsp.	gingerroot grated
1/4 tsp.	nutmeg
1/4 tsp.	dried dill flakes
1 tbsp.	sesame oil
1 tbsp.	butter
	salt & pepper to taste

1. Clean and prepare shrimp as per page 108. Set aside.
2. Melt butter with the sesame oil in a frying pan over medium heat.
3. Add onion, garlic, gingerroot, and fry for 2 minutes.
4. Add shrimp and fry for 3 to 10 minutes.
5. Add rest of ingredients and bring to a boil.
6. Reduce heat and simmer for 5 minutes.

Suggestion: Serve over rice. Serves 4-8.

Mussels over Pasta

2 lbs.	mussels in the shell
1/2 cup	black olives sliced
1/2 cup	green olives sliced
2 cups	stewed tomatoes loosely chopped with their juice
1 cup	zucchini thinly sliced
1 cup	mushrooms thinly sliced
1 cup	sweet onion diced
450g pasta	(e.g. spaghetti, linguine, or fettuccini) cooked
1 tbsp.	olive oil
1 tbsp.	soya sauce
1 tbsp.	worcestershire sauce
1 cup	chicken stock
1/2 cup	apple juice

1. Clean and prepare mussels as per page 138.
2. Sauté onion in oil for 1 minute, add mushrooms, and tomatoes, cook for 2 minutes over high heat.
3. Lower heat to medium and add zucchini, olives, soya sauce, worcestershire sauce, chicken stock and apple juice. Simmer for 10 minutes.
4. Add mussels and cook covered over low heat until mussels open. Discard any that do not open.
5. Pour sauce over freshly cooked hot pasta. Sprinkle with parmesan or maybe some crumbled feta cheese.

Serves 4-6.

Mussels are low in fat and carbohydrates. They are a great source of protein, vitamins and minerals that are important to our diet.

Full Meal Deal Skewers

1 lb.	new red and white potatoes (small in size)
1 lb.	corn on the cob
1 lb.	zucchini
1 lb.	green peppers
1 lb.	red peppers
1 lb.	sweet onions
1 lb.	boneless chicken breast
1 lb.	pork
1 lb.	beef
1 lb.	small whole mushrooms
1 lb.	medium sized shrimp cleaned, de-veined
2 cups	Italian style salad dressing

1. Parboil potatoes for 5 minutes in salted water.
2. Make sure all food pieces are the same size so they cook evenly. Cut the vegetables into 1 inch pieces and the meat in half or one inch cubes. The bigger the food pieces, the longer it will take to cook.
3. Thread food on skewers starting with a vegetable, then a piece of meat or seafood, then another vegetable making sure each skewer has one of each of the items.
4. Place skewers in a shallow baking pan and coat with Italian salad dressing. Let sit for 15 minutes in refrigerator.
5. Remove skewers from marinade.
6. Place skewers on barbecue or in the oven at 375°F on a cookie sheet.
7. Baste with marinade as they cook.
8. Cook until shrimp are pink and curled tightly, approx. 10 to 20 minutes.

Serves 4-10.

Leek and Salmon Pizza

one	12" pizza crust
1 cup	leeks* sliced thinly and round
1 cup	soft cheese like cottage, goat, or cream cheese at room temperature
1 tsp.	dill dried flakes
1 tsp.	cumin powder
1 cup	plum tomatoes medium diced
1 tsp.	basil flakes
1 lb.	smoked salmon sliced very thinly or flaked apart
1/2 cup	mozzarella cheese grated
1 tbsp.	olive oil
1 tbsp.	sesame seeds
1/4 cup	sesame oil
	salt & pepper to taste

1. Spread 1 tbsp. olive oil on the pizza pan and spread out dough creating a crust on the outside edge.
2. Make sure cheese is very soft. Spread over pizza dough. (Soften the cheese by microwaving if necessary.)
3. Sprinkle all herbs over evenly. Add salmon, and then layer on tomatoes, leeks, and mozzarella cheese.
4. Brush the edge of the crust with sesame oil and dust with seeds. Drizzle any left over sesame oil over top of cheese.
5. Bake at 375°F until golden and bubbly.

Serves 4-6.

***Leeks:** Cleaning a leek is very easy. Slice the leek down from top to the bottom in both directions to just about 1 inch above the root, and rotate and cut again making an X. This will allow you to fan it out under cold running water to remove any dirt or you can chop it up and place it in a strainer to remove the dirt. Leeks grow up through the sand thus dirt collects inside their layered leaves. If using longer strips to hold hors d'oeuvre style items, cut pieces and wash gentle piece by piece in cold water to ensure sand and dirt have been removed.

Lobster with Creamed Peas

2 lbs.	lobster meat
2 lbs.	sweet garden peas cleaned and shelled
1 tsp.	dill
1 tsp.	worcestershire sauce
1 tsp.	soya sauce
1/4 cup	lemon juice
zest	of 1 lemon
1/2 cup	onion minced
1/2 cup	sour cream
	salt & pepper to taste

1. Cook peas in salted boiling water until tender, approximately 3 to 10 minutes. Drain well.
2. Stir all remaining ingredients in a deep pot until all is coated and evenly mixed. Cook over medium heat until lobster is hot.

Suggestion: Serve as a main dish over rice, noodles or in a pastry shell. Serve as a side dish to larger seafood dish. Serve hot or at room temperature. Great for barbecues.

Serves 4-6.

Chinese Hot 'n Sour Shrimp Soup

2 lbs.	small raw shrimp in shell
2 cups	spinach julienned
dash	of dill
rind	of a whole lemon
rind	of a whole lime
1/4 cup	lemon juice
1 tbsp.	fresh gingerroot grated
1 cup	chicken stock
2 cups	shrimp or lobster stock
1/4 cup	green onion minced
1/2 tsp.	dried basil powder
1/2 cup	sweet red pepper diced
1/2 cup	sweet yellow pepper diced
1/2 cup	jalapeno pepper sliced thinly
1/2 cup	pineapple juice
1/2 cup	pineapple crushed
1 tbsp.	soya sauce
1 tbsp.	worcestershire sauce
1 tsp.	sesame oil or sesame seeds
	water to cover
	salt & pepper to taste

...continued on next page

1. Clean and prepare shrimp as per instructions page 108.
2. Place all ingredients except the shrimp and the sesame oil/seeds, in a large deep pot. Cover with water so that the water level is always 2 inches above the food at all times.
3. Bring to a boil and let simmer on low for 20 minutes. Add sesame oil, seeds, and shrimp, let cook until shrimp are pink and curled tightly, approximately 5 minutes.
4. Serve piping hot.

Serves 4.

For an added flair you may leave the shrimp whole with the shell on, for a rustic hands on style of soup.

dulse

Seaweed is high in potassium, calcium, and iron; it is also considered to be a natural detoxifier. Rumor has it, that seaweed reduces the gaseous attributes in foods like beans and cabbage. Seaweed is defined by some as wet and fresh, just picked, while the sun cured version is often referred to as dulse.

Hawaiian Shrimp Skewers

24	large tiger shrimp
8	skewers sticks or rods
16	chunks of fresh pineapple in 1 inch cubes
16	peach halves (pits removed)

1. Clean and prepare shrimp as per instructions, page 108.
2. Thread skewers as follows: peach, shrimp, pineapple, shrimp, peach, shrimp, and finishing with pineapple.
3. Grill on barbecue over medium heat until fruit softens slightly and shrimp are plump and curled, about 10 to 20 minutes.

Suggestion: Serve with fruit relish (recipe follows below), a salad of lightly wilted warmed greens like Swiss chard or spinach; and accompanied with a sweet rice like jasmine or basmati.

Serves 4-8

Fruit Relish

1/2 cup	ripe mango diced
1/2 cup	avocado diced
1/2 cup	kiwi diced
2 tbsps.	lime juice
2 tbsps.	lemon juice
1/4 cup	onion finely minced
1 tsp.	garlic minced
1 tsp.	worcestershire sauce
	salt & pepper to taste

...continued on next page

1. Place all ingredients into a small saucepan and heat on grill or stove top until it comes to a boil. Cook for two minutes more, stirring often. Remove from heat and pour over skewers.

Makes approx. 1 to 1 ½ cups.

When using wooden skewers, soak them in water for at least 30 minutes before use. This will prevent them from burning and flaring up during the cooking process. The water also makes the skewers a little softer, so be gentle when piercing food pieces, as they can break off.

Cut wooden sticks in half for appetizer size skewers.

Metal skewer rods usually hold more food as they are generally bigger in size. The metal version also heats from the inside out and continues to hold its temperature for a few minutes once removed from the heat source so food stays warm longer.

Choose which style is more convenient for you and your dish.

The SCUBA (Self Contained Underwater Breathing Apparatus) tank as it is known, was invented in NB by James Elliott & Alexander McAvity in 1839. This holding tank of air for divers made it very easy to gather scallops from the cold waters. Divers could stay underwater longer, thus collecting more scallops.

Salmon and Scallop Tartare

1/2 lb.	salmon, boneless raw
1/2 lb.	baby scallops, raw
1/4 tsp.	dill
1/2 tsp.	lemon juice
	salt & pepper to taste

1. Mince salmon and scallops finely by hand.
2. Massage the dill, lemon juice and pepper in by hand.
3. Toss with a sprinkle of sea salt.

Variation: Try adding 1 to 2 tbsps. of licorice flavoured liquor such as Pernod or Anisette.

Suggestion: Serve cold on crispy toasts with a drop of sour cream.

Fish oil is a food supplement known for its high content of vitamin A & D. It was recognized and invented in the daily dose form in 1921 by Hartley Wentworth from Deer Island. The popularity of its health benefits grew so large and quickly that the Famous Ganong Brothers Limited Chocolate Factory played with ideas to add chocolate to make it appealing to small children.

Sweet Summer Salmon Salsa

1 lb.	of salmon cleaned, cooked, broken into bite sized morsels
1	firm ripe avocado diced small
1/2 cup	red onion minced
1 tbsp.	dill
1 tsp.	cayenne pepper
	salt & pepper to taste
1/2 cup	mandarin oranges drained, loosely chopped with juice reserved
1 tbsp.	soya sauce
1 tbsp.	worcestershire sauce

1. Mix mandarin juice, soya sauce, and worcestershire sauce in a bowl and set aside.
2. Mix everything else in a deep bowl until evenly combined.
3. Pour sauce over salad and re-toss.

Suggestion: Serve on a bed of rice or lettuce, or toss with cold pasta. This recipe may also be used as a vegetable or chip dip, or heated and used as a sauce for angel hair pasta.

Makes approx. 3 cups.

Succulent Shrimp Marinara

2 lbs.	shrimp
1 tsp.	dill
1 tsp.	garlic minced
1 tsp.	olive oil
1 cup	tomato sauce
1 cup	onion finely minced
1 tsp.	basil powder
1 cup	celery finely minced
1 tbsp.	worcestershire sauce
1 tbsp.	soya sauce
1/2 cup	feta or soft goat cheese crumbled
1/2 cup	oil soaked sun dried tomatoes finely minced
1 cup	scalding hot boiled water
450g	flat wide egg noodles
	salt & pepper to taste

1. Boil water and pour over the sun dried tomatoes in a bowl, cover and set aside. Let soak for 30 minutes, Drain water into the sauce pot. Finely mince or purée tomatoes. Set aside.
2. Fry onions, celery, and basil in the oil until slightly golden in colour.
3. Add shrimp and garlic, then fry until they start turning pink. Add the tomato sauce, worcestershire sauce, soya sauce, and fresh basil. Bring to a boil and then reduce heat to a simmer. Let simmer until you cook the pasta.
4. Cook pasta according to package directions.
5. Pour shrimp and sauce over pasta. Sprinkle with cheese.

Serves 4-6.

Sailor's Breakfast Omelette

1/2 lb.	maple cured bacon, thickly sliced
1/2 cup	salmon (cooked, cooled and flaked apart)
1 tbsp.	chives
1 cup	cooked potatoes, cubed or mashed
3	large eggs beaten
1/2 cup	cheddar cheese grated
1 tbsp.	maple syrup
	salt & pepper to taste

1. Fry bacon until crispy. Drain and reserve fat.
2. Break bacon into bite size pieces. Set aside.
3. Beat eggs until frothy, add salt and pepper.
4. Add maple syrup, salmon, and potatoes, re-stir until evenly mixed.
5. Pour mixture into a frying pan over medium to high heat.
6. Stir for 1 minute and then let rest, covering immediately and reducing heat to low.
7. Let omelette cook for 2 to 3 minutes. Add bacon, chives and top with cheese. Cover again and turn off heat.
8. As soon as cheese is melted serve piping hot.

Serves 1-2.

Crab Caesar Salad

2 lbs.	cooked crab with juice reserved
1/2 cup	Creamy Caesar Salad Dressing recipe (page 59)
1 head	of romaine lettuce
1 cup	of croutons*
1/4 cup	parmesan cheese grated
1 tsp.	lemon juice
1 tbsp.	worcestershire sauce
1 tsp.	dill flakes
1/4 cup	bacon bits
	lemon wedges
	salt & pepper to taste

1. Clean and wash romaine lettuce, cut into bite size pieces. Set aside.
2. Prepare crab, cut into 1/2" cubes. Set aside in fridge until ready to use.
3. In a deep mixing bowl, stir the caesar dressing, worcestershire sauce, lemon juice, parmesan cheese, salt, dill, and pepper together until mixed evenly.
4. Add in the crab meat, toss well to coat all meat. Add lettuce, croutons, and bacon bits. Toss well and serve. Garnish with lemon wedges.

Variations: This recipe can be made with any flavour of shellfish or seafood.
By the Shore Shrimp Caesar – add 2 lbs. baby shrimp.
Atlantic Lobster Caesar Salad – add 2 lbs. lobster meat (knuckles, claws, tail).
Zesty Salmon Caesar – add 2 lbs. cooked salmon chunks.

*Croutons – try one of the recipes on page 58.

A lobsters' biggest claw is called the "crusher". The smaller claw is called a "pincher" claw, usually used for holding food, assisting the crusher claw. Lobsters with only one claw or no claws are called "culls", they are usually available at a lower price.

When at the local fish market selecting your lobster for tonight's meal, choose the female of the species as they are usually larger, contain more meat and are sweeter to the taste than the male counterpart. If the internal roe (eggs) is still intact, it may be reserved for a garnish on the salad, or in soup or on crackers.

In order to preserve the lobster industry, all fishermen who find a female lobster bearing eggs externally (referred to as berried), with her underside covered in bright red roe, must release the female back into the water. This is not a good deed but a law in order to protect the livelihood of the many fishermen and to maintain the industry.

Most scientists say lobsters have no cerebral cortex (the area of the brain that gives the perception of pain), thus they do not feel pain. Lobsters do not have vocal cords so they do not scream when you cook them. There is sometimes a hissing sound as steam escapes from their shell.

Shediac, NB is known as the lobster capital of the world. When visiting New Brunswick, travel to nearby Moncton during the month of August for their famous Atlantic Seafood Festival, it gets bigger every year.

Parmesan Fried Scallops

64	baby scallops (8 per skewer)
16	long slices of bacon
16	skewer rods
1	lemon
1 cup	fresh parmesan cheese grated
1/2 cup	fresh, dry, fine bread crumbs
	salt & pepper to taste

1. Mix cheese, bread crumbs, salt & pepper together in a bowl until even.
2. Place crumbs on a cookie sheet and spread them out, you will be rolling the completed skewers in the crumbs.
3. Weave 8 baby scallops on a skewer with a strip of bacon, weaving the bacon in between each scallop.
4. Roll each skewer in the crumb mixture coating as much as possible.
5. Broil in the oven or bake on high heat on the barbecue until bacon is crispy. Approx. 5 to 20 minutes.
6. Sprinkle with fresh lemon* juice before serving.

*Any citrus juice may be used, lime, orange, etc.

Serve 4-8 (produces 8 skewers).

Sweet 'n Spicy Grilled Pita with Seafood

2	large scallops
2	large tiger shrimp
1	large round slice of fresh pineapple
3	baby tomatoes
1/4 cup	brown sugar
1/4 cup	jalapeno green tabasco sauce*
1/4 cup	shredded lettuce
1/4 cup	cheese of choice grated
1 tbsp.	olive oil
1	large pita pocket or tortilla
	salt & pepper to taste

1. Place everything but the lettuce and cheese in a bowl and toss well to make sure all is coated.
2. Over high heat, grill the scallops, shrimp, baby tomatoes, and pineapple until golden in color. Be careful that your tomatoes do not explode, keep them to the side on lower heat.
3. Dip pita in cold water and place on the grill for 1 minute per side.
4. Place all into the pita or tortilla and serve with lettuce and cheese on top.

***Note:** Start with 1/2 tsp. hot sauce and continue to add until desired hotness is achieved.

Serves 1.

Codfish Morning Crumpets

4	cod fillets
4	crumpets
1/4 cup	onion finely minced
1 cup	cheddar cheese grated
4 tbsps.	cream cheese
2 tbsps.	oil (vegetable or olive)
	salt & pepper to taste

1. Fry cod fillets in oil until cooked using medium to high heat. Drain on paper towel and set aside.
2. Drain oil from pan and fry onion until tender. Remove from heat.
3. Slice crumpets in half round wise. Toast crumpets and set aside.
4. On a cookie sheet, spread out 4 bottom halves of the crumpets.
5. Spread 1 tbsp. of cream cheese on each crumpet.
6. Spoon onion over top of the cheese.
7. Place a fish portion on top of the onion and top with cheddar cheese.
8. Broil in oven until cheese is bubbly. Top with the other half of the crumpet.

Variation: Try a flavoured cream cheese or change the cheddar to your favourite cheese.

Suggestion: Try placing some scrambled egg on the top half and serve open faced. Be extravagant and serve cheese or hollandaise sauce over top.

Serves 4.

Chapter Four

Desserts

Ok! just one more bite

Best Blueberry Muffins

The key to making these muffins is the flour that coats the blueberries. It prevents them from sinking to the bottom. ***This recipe is a Basic Muffin recipe****, to use for another flavour of muffins just omit the blueberries.*

1 cup	white sugar
1 cup	blueberries cleaned*
1/2 cup	milk slightly warmed
3 tbsps.	melted butter
2	eggs
2 tsps.	baking powder
1 tsp.	vanilla
1 ½ cups + 2 tbsps. flour	
dash	of salt

1. Place berries in a bowl by themselves and add the 2 tbsps. of flour. Stir gently until all flour is absorbed. Be careful not to crush the berries.
2. Mix all of the ingredients except the berries in a deep mixing bowl until dough is even and smooth. It takes about 7 minutes by hand or 4 with electric mixer. Gently fold in the blueberries.
3. Bake at 375° F for 35 to 50 minutes or until top of cake springs back or cake tester is clear.

Variation: *Cranberries, pineapple, apple, strawberries, etc, may be used in place of or in combination with the blueberries.

Blueberry muffins are a favourite in many maritime kitchens. This recipe is from my first cookbook titled : "A Taste of New Brunswick, recipes from our kitchens" August 2001 Neptune Publishing Company Ltd. ISBN : 1-896270-17-4.

Harvest Time Applesauce

5 lbs.	apples cored, peeled & cut in pieces
1/2 cup	water
1/2 tsp.	cinnamon
dash	of nutmeg

1. Place all in a pot and stir well.
2. Cover and cook on low heat for 30 minutes stirring often, until fruit has become soft.

Variation: Add some other fruit such as pears, plums, peaches, blueberries, apricots or cranberries.

Suggestion: Serve warm in a bowl with whipped cream for dessert, as a condiment with or over lamb or pork dishes, or a hot breakfast cereal. It also makes a great topping for ice cream.

Note: The longer you cook the apples the browner in colour they get as they oxidize with the air and heat. This is called Apple Butter, and is sweeter than cooking for just the original 30 minutes in the recipe.

Apple picking is a tradition as well as a livelihood for many New Brunswickers. It's easy to get carried away at many of the U-pick orchards and arrive home with more apples than you can eat. Applesauce is the perfect answer for the over-enthusiastic apple picker.

Crumble Mixture

1 cup	oatmeal (minute oats)
1 cup	flour
3/4 cup	brown sugar
1/2 cup	butter at room temperature

1. In a deep mixing bowl, add oatmeal, flour, brown sugar and mix until even.
2. Rub in softened butter by hand or cut in with pastry cutter until the mixture turns into a rough lumpy dough. Dough should clump together loosely. Make sure that all the flour is incorporated. If mixture is too sticky add a little more flour.
3. Bake at 350°F until crunchy and golden brown.

Suggestion: Use as a topping on desserts, pies, cakes, muffins or to make apple crumble.

Lemon Buttercream Frosting

1/2 cup	butter
1/2 cup	margarine (block style)
1 tbsp.	lemon juice
2 tsps.	lemon zest
4 cups	icing sugar sifted

1. Mix butter and margarine until creamed.
2. Add lemon juice and zest. Re-mix until smooth.
3. Add icing sugar 1 cup at a time until all is absorbed and the frosting is smooth.

Makes approx. 3 cups.

Golden Sweet Fruit Bake

1 cup	raspberries
2 cups	blueberries
1 cup	strawberries
2 cups	rhubarb
1/2 cup	brown sugar
1 tbsp.	vanilla
1/2 tsp.	cinnamon
1/4 tsp.	nutmeg
1/4 tsp.	ground cloves
1 recipe	Crumble Mixture recipe (page 172)

1. Make Crumble Mixture recipe and set aside.
2. Wash berries well. Cut strawberries in half and rhubarb into 1 inch chunks.
3. Place the fruit into a 9" x 13" baking dish, making sure the berries are evenly mixed.
4. Sprinkle with brown sugar, cinnamon, nutmeg, vanilla and cloves.
5. Sprinkle top with Crumble Mixture.
6. Place baking dish on a cookie sheet.
7. Bake at 325°F until golden and bubbly, approx. 30 to 45 minutes.

Suggestion: Serve with homemade whipped cream, or maple ice cream.

Serve 6-10.

Grilled Pineapple Wedges

1	large pineapple
1/2 cup	lime juice
1 tbsp.	lemon juice
1 cup	brown sugar
1/2 tsp.	cinnamon
1 tbsp.	mint leaves minced
	pepper to taste

1. Clean, peel and slice pineapple into thick wedges or 1 inch thick round slices. Place wedges in a shallow baking dish.
2. Mix lemon juice, lime juice, pepper, cinnamon, and mint in a bowl until combined.
3. Spread mixture over pineapple wedges. Let sit for 5 minutes.
4. Remove from sauce, sprinkle with brown sugar.
5. Place on a cookie sheet and broil until golden brown in colour.

Suggestion: Serve with a fresh salad or as a dessert with maple ice cream.

Serves 4-8.

Cranberry Orange Muffins

1	Basic Muffin recipe (page170)
2 tbsps.	orange juice
1 tbsp.	orange flavouring*
3 tbsps.	orange zest finely minced
1 cup	fresh cranberries mashed
1/4 tsp.	cinnamon
1/4 tsp.	nutmeg
1 tbsp.	vanilla

1. Mix all well in a deep mixing bowl. Bake in lined muffin tins according to the muffin recipe instructions.

Variation: Try adding 1/2 cup raisins or walnuts.

*Flavouring is optional.

Makes 12 to 24 muffins.

Hint: For a tell tale sign of the flavour of the muffins, place a small piece of the fruit on the top of each muffin before baking. For example, a blueberry for blueberry muffins, or for this recipe, try a curl of orange zest and a cranberry on top slightly pushed into the batter before baking.

Maple Buttercream Crunch Frosting

1 tbsp.	maple flavouring*
1 tbsp.	vanilla
1/2 cup	butter
1/2 cup	margarine (block style)
1/4 cup	real maple syrup
4 cups	icing sugar sifted
1/4 tsp.	cinnamon
1	Skor bar crushed

1. Mix butter and margarine until creamed.
2. Add maple, vanilla, maple syrup, cinnamon and beat until absorbed.
3. Add icing sugar one cup at a time until all is absorbed.
4. Thin with cold water.
5. Once desired consistency is reached, crush the Skor bar finely and stir it in.

*Flavouring optional.

Hint: Maple syrup varies from light (mild) to medium (amber) to dark(strong). The stronger the maple syrup the more pronounced the flavour in your recipe.

Makes approx. 3 cups.

Sweet Lemon Mint Glaze

2 cups	icing sugar sifted well
1/2 cup	lemon juice
1 tsp.	lemon zest
1 tbsp.	mint leaves minced

1. Mix all of the above in a bowl until evenly mixed. Thin with additional lemon juice if desired.

Suggestion: Try it poured on cakes, cookies, pies, toast, scones, and fresh fruit or serve as a dip for kabobs. The sauce will be shiny and will harden only slightly once it air dries.

Makes approx. 1 to 1 ½ cups.

Orange Buttercream Frosting

1/2 cup	butter
1/2 cup	margarine (block style)
1 tbsp.	orange juice
2 tbsps.	orange zest
4 cups	icing sugar sifted

1. Mix butter and margarine until creamed.
2. Add orange juice and zest, re-mix until smooth.
3. Add icing sugar, mixing in 1 cup at a time until all is absorbed and smooth.
4. Can be made by hand or with a mixer. Thin with cold water 1 tbsp. at a time.

Makes approx. 3 cups.

Cinnamon Butter Frosting

1/2 cup	butter
1/2 cup	margarine (block style)
4 cups	icing sugar sifted
3 tbsps.	vanilla
2 tbsps.	cinnamon
1 tsp.	honey

1. Beat butter, margarine, vanilla, cinnamon, and honey until butter is creamed.
2. Add icing sugar 1 cup at a time. Use cold water by the tbsp. to thin.

Suggestion: Great over bran muffins, carrot cake, pound cake or oatcakes.

Makes approx. 3 cups.

Cinnamon Oil

2 cups	oil*
1/2 cup	cinnamon powder

1. Heat oil over medium heat for 5 minutes. Add cinnamon and continue heating for another 5 minutes. Strain through cheesecloth once cooled.
2. Store in fridge for 1 month.

Suggestion: Use over pastry before baking. Spread on the top of an uncooked pie crust. Use in recipes where oil is called for; pancakes, eggs, bacon, ham, sausages, potato cakes, fish, chicken or just about anything else that cinnamon can enhance. Use it as a dessert topping for oatmeal in the morning.

***Oil:** Use olive oil preferably as this is such a versatile oil for both cooking and eating. Any oil may be used.

Makes approx. 2 cups.

Grandma's Baked Apples

4	large apples (variety of choice but not a soft apple like Red or Golden Delicious)
1/2 cup	apple juice
1	Crumble Mixture recipe (page 172)
1/2 tsp.	cinnamon
1/2 tsp.	nutmeg

1. Wash apples and remove core.
2. Place apples in a shallow baking dish.
3. Pour 1/2 cup apple juice into the pan.
4. Mix Crumble Mixture with cinnamon and nutmeg.
5. Add Crumble Mixture to cored out apples and bake.
6. Bake at 350°F until golden and juices bubble. Apple will pierce easily once tender. Approx. 20 to 45 minutes.

Serves 4.

Raspberry Maple Syrup

1 cup	maple syrup
1 cup	raspberries
1 tsp.	cinnamon
1 tsp.	nutmeg
	pinch of salt

1. Pour syrup into a deep bowl. Add all remaining ingredients and stir until evenly mixed.

Suggestion: Serve hot or cold, using right away or store in fridge for 1 month in a sealed jar. Goes great over oatmeal, pancakes or French toast. Try on ice cream, cheesecakes, or pies.

Variation: Substitute one or a combination of the fruits listed below, adding the same measurement of 1 cup of fruit.
Blueberry Maple Sauce – add 1 cup fresh blueberries mashed, or frozen (thaw first).
Strawberry Maple Sauce – add 1 cup fresh strawberries mashed, or frozen (thaw first).
Cranberry Maple Syrup – add 1 cup cranberries freshly mashed, or frozen (thaw first).
Autumn Apple Maple Syrup – add 1 cup applesauce.

Makes approx. 2 cups.

Best Blueberry Grunt

1	Dough Boys recipe (page 70)
4 cups	blueberries cleaned
1/4 cup	water
1 tbsp.	lemon juice
1/4 cup	white or brown sugar

1. Place all of the above in a medium sized pot.
2. Cover and cook slowly over low heat until mixture is almost jam. (About 20 to 45 minutes).
2. Drop the dumplings into the jam. Push dumplings about half way under the jam.
3. Cover the pot; cook on low heat for 15 minutes.

Suggestion: Serve the dumplings with some of the jam poured over top and for an added touch add whipped cream, ice cream, sorbet, custard or tapioca spooned over top.

Serves 4-8.

Chapter Four

Blueberries, blueberries, blueberries… so abundant, they are New Brunswick's number one fruit crop in volume of production and export. This crop is the livelihood of many local families. New Brunswick's hillsides are covered in blues, purples, crimson and reds during August to mid September as the fields ripen for the harvest. Many students are hired just for blueberry raking season. Roadside stands pop up everywhere and blueberry pies compete at church suppers. You can find jams, jellies, pies, cakes, muffins, grunts, and sauces on the menu. Try some fresh from the U-picks or blueberry stands and make a pie sometime soon.

Sweet Cranberry Maple Pecan Tart

1	Princess Cheesecake batter recipe (page 195)
1	deep dish pie shell single layer only
2 tbsps.	white sugar
2 cups	cranberries
1 cup	chopped pecans
1 cup	slivered almonds
1/4 cup	maple syrup

1. Place pie dough in a tart pan and sprinkle crust with the white sugar.
2. Add maple syrup to the completed cheesecake batter, stirring until combined. Pour the cheesecake batter into the pan.
3. Spread the berries evenly over top of the cheesecake batter and lightly press them into the batter.
4. Spread the pecans on first, then the almonds, spreading them evenly across the top of the berries. Press them so they are covered by some of the cheesecake batter to prevent any burning.
5. Bake at 350°F for 30 to 45 minutes until cheesecake is slightly firm.

Suggestion: For an added touch, drizzle with a chocolate or caramel sauce once cooled.

Makes one 9 inch tart.

Blueberry Maple Drizzle

3 cups	blueberries*
1 cup	maple syrup
1/4 cup	brown sugar
1 cup	apple juice
1/2 tsp.	cinnamon
1 tbsp.	vanilla

1. Cook all in a deep pot over low to medium heat for 20 minutes stirring often.
2. Remove from heat and let cool for 5 minutes.

***Variations:** Add 3 cups of one or a combination of the following fruits: cranberry; raspberry; strawberry; apple; or blackberry in place of the blueberries. Fruit can be either jam; jelly; frozen (thaw first); or freshly mashed berries, or for apple, use Harvest Time Applesauce for best flavour results, see recipe page 171.

Suggestion: Serve hot or cold, use as a basting or stewing sauce for chicken, pork, beef, seafood, fruit or vegetables. Use as a variation of Maple Glazed Chicken Sauce see recipe page 83.

Makes approx. 5 cups.

Maple syrup is another industry within NB that we enjoy all year long. The season runs from early spring to early summer. Try a tour of one of the many sugar shacks to learn more about the harvesting and production of this delightful delicacy that makes many of our local desserts taste divine.

Apple Rhubarb Muffins

1	Basic Muffin recipe (page 170)
1/4 cup	oatmeal (minute oats)
1 tbsp. ea.	orange juice, lemon juice
1 tbsp.	lemon zest
1 tbsp.	orange zest
1 cup	apple pieces minced without peel
1 cup	rhubarb pieces thinly sliced
1 tsp. ea.	cinnamon, nutmeg
2 tbsps.	vanilla

1. Mix all well in a deep mixing bowl and bake in lined muffin tins according to the muffin recipe instructions.

Variation: Add 1/2 cup golden raisins, walnuts; or top with a streusel topping.

Strawberries are a very common but welcome berry of the summer. Strawberry shortcake and strawberry rhubarb combinations run rampant in pies, muffins, cakes and so much more during the strawberry season. NB boasts a 2 month strawberry season with local festivals, church suppers, barbecues and picnics all rejoicing in the delicious succulent and very juicy berry of summer. Try to plan your visit during this season; the fragrance of strawberry blossoms coming from farmers' fields will drive you wild as you travel across our beautiful province. The smells may entice you to stop at one of the local U-pick strawberry stands and enjoy a feed, or pick some to take with you. You can strike up a conversation with the farmer about the strawberry industry we have and, if you are lucky get invited to the farmhouse for a piece of fresh pie.

Raspberry Cream

2 cups	raspberries*
1 litre	cream**

*Fruit can be raspberry, strawberry, blueberry, cranberry, blackberry, or apple.

**Cream can be yogurt, coffee cream, cereal cream, whipping cream, buttermilk, soy milk or silken tofu.

1. Purée berries until smooth. You may strain through a fine sieve to remove seeds if desired.

2. Add cream and stir until smooth.

Suggestion: Serve over fiddleheads or asparagus; serve as a salad dressing or as a fruit dip. Bake chicken, fish or pork in it.

Makes approx. 5 cups.

Raspberries have been said to be a great source of vitamin C. They are healthy and grow abundantly in our maritime soil and climate. Usually available from mid July through August at farmers' markets, local roadside stands and a variety of U-pick farms. Not as popular as the common strawberry but as divine in flavour and favoured by many chefs for its wonderful compliment to chocolate.

Apple Oatmeal Deep Dish Pie

1 recipe	Grandma's Classic Oatmeal Cookies (page 192)
3 cups	thick Harvest Time Applesauce recipe (page 171)
1 can	sweetened condensed milk
2 cups	Skor bar crushed into small bits

1. Make cookie recipe and press it gently into a 9" x 13" ungreased casserole dish.
2. Spread applesauce on top of cookie dough.
3. Sprinkle toffee bits over top of the apple sauce.
4. Pour the sweetened condensed milk evenly over the top of the Skor bar pieces.
5. Bake on a cookie sheet at 350°F until cream and crust are golden. (Approx. 20 to 45 minutes).

Variation: Try using a variety of fruits in place of the apple, try blueberry, blueberry & applesauce mixed, pumpkin and applesauce mixed, pumpkin and cranberry mixed, or any variety that suits your taste buds.

Blue and Red Berry Pie a.k.a. Bumbleberry Pie

1	double Perfect Pie Crust recipe (page 193)
3 cups	strawberries sliced
3 cups	blueberries
1 cup	blackberries
1/2 cup	brown sugar
1 tsp.	cinnamon
1 tbsp.	lemon juice
dash	of salt
3 tbsps.	cornstarch

1. Mix all berries with brown sugar, cinnamon, lemon juice and salt in a bowl. Stir until all sugar has coated the berries and the sugar is mostly dissolved.
2. Place the bottom pie shell in an ungreased pie plate. Fill pie crust with berry mixture. Sprinkle cornstarch evenly over the top.
3. Add top crust, making a few vent holes.
4. Bake at 425°F until golden and juices bubble. (30 to 45 minutes).

Optional: Wash top of pie crust with a beaten egg mixed with 1 tbsp. of cold water and then sprinkle some sugar over crust before baking.

Makes 1 nine inch pie.

Autumn Apple Crisp

3 cups	white flour
6 cups	oatmeal
2 cups	margarine or butter at room temperature
3 cups	brown sugar
5 lbs.	of apples, cleaned, cored and thinly sliced (Macintosh or Cortland)
1/2 tsp.	cinnamon

1. Mix all dry ingredients well, and then rub in butter. Mix until crumbly, and all butter is absorbed.
2. Place half of the mixture in the bottom of an ungreased 9" x 13" pan. Press firmly but do not pack it down. Set aside.
3. Peel and core the apples.
4. Slice apples thinly and place in a deep pot over medium heat.
5. Add 1/2 cup water and cinnamon. Simmer until half cooked, stirring often.
6. Place cooked apple mixture on the top of the crumb mixture you have already pressed into the baking pan. Loosely add the top layer of the crumb mixture.
7. Bake at 350° F for 35 to 50 minutes until the top is golden brown.

Suggestion: Serve hot with a scoop of maple ice cream.

Serves 6-12.

Saint John is the oldest chartered city in Canada. It is also home to the oldest public museum in Atlantic Canada. The New Brunswick Museum has two buildings in Saint John, be sure to take in the historic and current exhibitions.

Lemon Blueberry Jam Bread

1/4 cup	butter or margarine
1 cup	brown sugar
1	egg
1/2 cup	applesauce
2 cups	white flour plus 2 tbsps.
1 tsp.	baking soda
1/2 tsp.	salt
1 tbsp.	vanilla
1/4 tsp.	nutmeg
1/2 tsp.	cinnamon
1 tsp.	lemon juice
2 tbsps.	lemon zest
2 cups	blueberries

1. Grease a loaf pan. To prevent formation of a thick crust, line the pan with brown paper followed by parchment paper or tinfoil. Grease paper and set aside.
2. Cream sugar and butter well. Add egg and cream again.
3. Add applesauce, lemon zest and lemon juice. Mix well.
4. Add everything else except blueberries and the 2 tbsps. of flour, mix well.

...continued on next page

5. In a separate bowl, coat blueberries in the 2 tbsps. of flour so they will stick in the batter rather than sink to the bottom. Gently fold coated blueberries into the batter.

6. Place in loaf pan and bake at 350°F for 1 hour or until cake tester comes out clean.

This can also be baked in a bundt pan or 9" x 9" cake pan.

7. If the top of the bread is getting too dark gently lay a piece of tinfoil over the top of the pan.

Suggestion: Serve with a dollop of lemon custard, blueberry jam, whipped cream, or maybe maple ice cream. This loaf bread makes a nice reward as a dessert after a hot day in the sun picking blueberries.

Blueberry Lemon Muffins

1	Basic Muffin recipe (page 170)
3 tbsps.	lemon zest
1 cup	fresh blueberries
1/4 tsp.	cinnamon
1/4 tsp.	nutmeg
1 tbsp.	vanilla

1. Mix all well in a deep mixing bowl and bake in lined muffin tins following muffin recipe instructions.

Variation: Add 1/2 cup raisins or walnuts, or top each muffin with 1/2 tsp. poppy seeds before baking.

Makes 12.

Blueberries are New Brunswick's largest fruit crop. Did you know that bumblebees are a natural pollinator for the blueberry plant?

Grandma's Classic Oatmeal Cookies

1 1/4 cups	butter
3/4 cup	brown sugar
1/2 cup	white sugar
1	egg
2 tsps.	vanilla
1 tsp.	baking soda
1 1/2 cups	flour
3 cups	oatmeal (quick or minute oats)

1. Cream together the butter and both sugars in a large deep bowl until smooth.
2. Add egg and mix well, re-creaming until egg is incorporated.
3. Add all remaining ingredients except for the oatmeal and mix until all the flour is incorporated into the wet ingredients.
4. Add oatmeal and stir until evenly mixed.
5. Drop by tablespoons onto an ungreased or lined cookie sheet and bake at 375°F for 8 to 15 minutes until slightly golden around the edges. Remove from oven and let cookies rest for 5 minutes before removing them from cookie sheet. Overcooking will result in hard crunchy cookies. These cookies should be crisp and crunchy on the edge and soft and chewy in the centers.

Store in an airtight container for 1 week.

Suggestion: Try adding 1 to 2 cups of chocolate chips, raisins, dried cranberries, dried cherries or dried blueberries; after the oatmeal has been incorporated.

Makes 24 to 30 medium sized cookies.

Perfect Pie Crust

2 cups	flour
3/4 cup	shortening
1 tsp.	salt
4 to 8 tbsps.	cold water

1. Place flour in a deep bowl and cut in shortening with pastry cutter or by hand.
2. Add salt and stir thoroughly.
3. Add cold water starting with 2 tbsps. until the dough forms into a rough ball.
4. Ensure the ball of pie dough is wrapped well in plastic. Place in fridge for 20 minutes to cool. If you flatten the dough into a thin circle before wrapping, it makes it much easier to roll out once cooled.

Use as required. Bake at 425°F until golden brown.

Uncooked pie dough will keep for 3 to 5 days in fridge or 1 month in the freezer.

The secret to good pie dough is not to handle it too much with your hands. Use a pastry cutter, and wooden spoons to mix it, or use a food processor to bind the dough together. Just pulse in the processor until dough forms small roughly shaped balls. Then gather dough into a big ball by hand before wrapping in plastic.

Makes one 9 inch pie layer.

Savoury Pie Crust

This crust is used for mainly meat pies. The cheese adds an extra touch of flavour to a savoury pot pie.

1 1/2 cups	flour
1/2 cup	old cheddar cheese grated
1/2 tsp.	salt
1/3 cup	cold butter
1/3 cup	cold lard
1/4 cup	cold water

1. In a large bowl, combine flour, cheese and salt. Using a pastry cutter or 2 knives, cut in the butter and lard until it resembles a loose crumbly matter and starts to clump together.
2. Add water 1 tbsp. at a time, gently kneading, until dough comes together into a ball.
3. Let sit in fridge covered in plastic wrap for 30 minutes.
4. Use as needed. Bake at 375°F to 425°F until crust is golden brown.

Makes one 9 inch pie crust.

Princess Cheesecake

2	8 ounce packages cream cheese (room temperature)
1/2 cup	sugar
2 tbsps.	vanilla
2	eggs (room temperature)
	pinch of salt

1. In a deep bowl, cream the cheese by hand or mixer until smooth, about 3 to 5 minutes.
2. Add sugar, vanilla and a pinch of salt, re-mix until incorporated.
3. Add eggs, and mix until they are evenly mixed throughout the batter.
4. Pour into a crust lined 8" springform pan.
5. Bake at 350°F for 25 to 40 minutes until the centre of the cake is still jiggly. Remove from oven and let sit until cool. Refrigerate for 6 hours before removing the cheesecake from the springform pan.

Makes one 8 inch cheesecake.

Variation: Try this cheesecake with a graham cracker crust (recipe on box of graham crackers), or try it on shortbread or gingersnap crust.

Gingersnap Cookie Crust

This recipe can be used in place of the traditional graham cracker crust called for in a recipe.

2 cups	gingersnap cookie crumbs
6 tbsps.	butter

1. Crush cookies by hand or in food processor until they turn into a fine cookie crumb.
2. Melt butter and add to crumbs, mixing until all butter is incorporated.
3. Press gently into a cookie pan and use as required.
4. Bake at 325°F for 12 to 15 minutes. Too long will result in a burnt cookie, be careful.

Note: If using in a recipe that calls for baking the dessert, there is no need to pre-cook your crust.

Makes one 9 inch crust.

Chocolate Chocolate Sauce

2/3 cup	icing sugar
2 tbsps.	cocoa
1 tsp.	vanilla
3 to 4 tsps.	water

1. Mix all in a bowl until smooth.

Suggestion: Drizzle over desserts.

Makes approx. 2/3 cup.

Layered Banana Supreme Cake

1	banana bread recipe
1 box	commercial banana instant pudding
1	Chocolate Chocolate Sauce recipe (page 196)
1	ripe banana
1 cup	whipped cream optional

1. Make banana bread according to recipe but bake it in two 8" round or square pans.
2. Let cakes cool. Dig out a cavity, removing about 1/4 of the top of each cake, leaving one inch border around the outside edge. Set aside.
3. Make instant pudding according to package. Add scraped out banana bread pieces and let set in fridge until firm.
4. On a cake plate, place one of the cake layers. Add half of the instant pudding to the hole you have dug out. Place the second layer of the cake on the first one. Add the remaining pudding bread mixture into the top of the second cake layer. Slice the banana and place over top for decoration. Place cake in fridge to set for 20 minutes.
5. Make chocolate sauce and pour evenly over the top allowing it to run down the sides of the cake.

If you are serving the cake right away, add some whipped cream on top.

Makes 1 double layer 8" cake.

Founded in 1873, in St. Stephen, NB. Ganong Brothers Limited is a world famous chocolate company. In 1855, Ganong launched their Christmas classic, chicken bone candy which is still famous for its hard pink candy with hints of cinnamon outside with a soft chocolate center. In 1889, Gilbert Ganong came up with the method to imprint and emboss initials on the bottom of hand made chocolates. Ganong also invented the world's first chocolate bar in 1910.

Conversion Chart

Measurement	Equivalent Measurements		
1 tsp.	5 ml.		
1 tbsp.	15 ml.	3 tsps.	1/2 oz.
1/8 cup	25 ml.	6 tsps.	1 oz or 2 tbsps.
1/4 cup	50 ml.	2ozs.	4 tbsps. or 12 tsps.
1/3 cup	75 ml.		
1/2 cup	125 ml.	4ozs.	8 tbsps. or 24 tsps.
2/3 cup	150 ml.		
3/4 cup	175 ml.		
1 cup or 1/2 pint	250 ml.	8ozs.	16 tbsps.
1/4 lb.	125g.		
1 lb.	454g.	16ozs.	
1000 ml.	1 litre	4 cups	
1 kg.	2.27 lbs.	1000gms.	
30 ml.	1oz.		
1/4 tsp.	1 ml.		
2 cups	1 pint		
2 pints or 1 litre	1 quart	4 cups	32ozs. or 1000 ml.
4 quarts	1 gallon	16 cups	
Pinch	1/8 tsp. or less		
1 peck	8 quarts		
1 bushel	4 pecks		
Jigger	1.5ozs.	3 tbsps.	

Abbreviation Definitions

tsp. = teaspoon
tbsp. = tablespoon
ml. = milliliter
oz. = ounce
g. = gram
gms. = grams
kg. = kilogram
lb. = pound

Cooking Temperature Guide For Various Meats

Ingredient	Fahrenheit	Celsius
Beef medium	145 to 160°F	63 to 72°C
Beef medium rare	130 to 145°F	55 to 63°C
Beef well done	170°F	77°C
Chicken, whole	180°F	83°C
Duck and Goose	180°F	83°C
Eggs	160°F	71°C
Ground Turkey, Chicken	165°F	74°C
Ham	160°F	71°C
Lamb medium	160°F	71°C
Lamb medium rare	145°F	63°C
Lamb well done	170°F	77°C
Pork medium	160°F	71°C
Pork well done	170°F	77°C
Poultry stuffed	170°F	77°C
Poultry thighs, wings	180°F	83°C
Turkey, whole	180°F	83°C

These temperatures are a guide and not guaranteed, check out the consumer board or association for the type of meat you are cooking for complete accuracy; make sure to use your meat thermometer in the thickest part of any food you are cooking. Most local butchers and grocery stores will also carry literature about the temperatures for each type of meat, drop by and ask for a guide.

About the Author

Karen's favourite place to be has been the kitchen. She has been in the cooking industry since finishing high school, motivated by an interest in all things food related. Her first cookbook was published in 2001 and will be in its fourth printing in 2006.

Karen is also interested in the creative aspects of her cooking involving cake decorating and contests. She was the Ocean Spray Canada's 2002 Atlantic Provinces Regional Winner and also was chosen as an entrant for The Breast Cancer Society of Canada 2001 Best Recipe of the Century Cookbook.

Karen's specialty is desserts, but she also excels in main courses especially those she shares at family get-togethers. Sometimes, there are as many as 100 or more people during the family summer potlucks; the menu always includes several of Karen's delicious creations.

November 2003 marked the launch of her first commercial food product, Karen's Chocolate Sauce, available at stores near you. If you live in Karen's home city of Saint John, New Brunswick, you may have sampled her well known shortbread cookies, or eaten at one of the restaurants where she was a cook. Karen's success at kitchen consulting gives her the opportunity to outsource her sweets to local businesses that wish to provide their customers with locally made food with natural ingredients.

She is currently developing various retail food products and hopes to present them in the near future. Her plans also include a cookbook for parents and children, which will focus on sharing the cooking experience while producing healthy meals that make food fun and interesting for children.

Index by Subject / Ingredient

BISQUES, CHOWDERS, SOUPS & STEWS

BREADS, RICE, BEANS & PASTA

CONDIMENTS, CHUTNEYS, DIPS, DUNKS, GRAVY, MARINADES, SALAD DRESSINGS, SALSAS, SAUCES, SPREADS

DESSERTS

Muffins

Pies & Tarts

Other

EGGS, CHEESE & BREAKFAST

FRUIT

Apple

Blackberry

Blueberry

Cranberry

SALADS

SEAFOOD

Cod

Crab

Lobster

Mussels

Oysters